THE HEALING POWER

Books by J Bernard Hutton

Danger From Moscow
Frogman Extraordinary
School for Spies
Stalin – The Miraculous Georgian
The Traitor Trade
Out Of This World
Healing Hands
Commander Crabb Is Alive
Struggle In The Dark
The Fake Defector
Hess – The Man And His Mission
The Great Illusion
On The Other Side Of Reality
Women Spies
The Subverters Of Liberty

Co-authored
The Private Life Of Josif Stalin
The Pain And The Glory – The Life Of Smetana

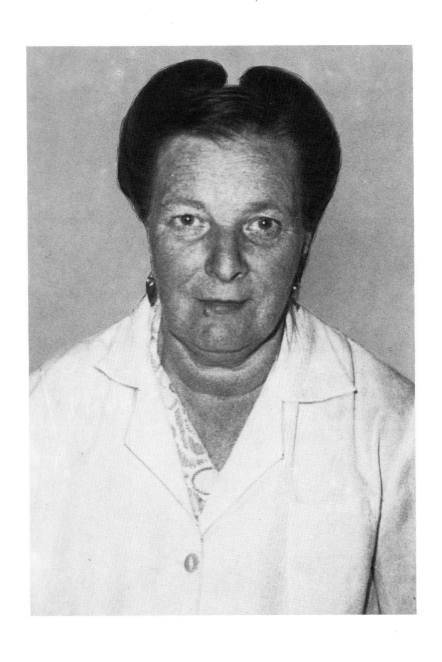

Mrs. Leah Doctors

THE HEALING POWER

The Extraordinary Spiritual Healing of Mrs. Leah Doctors and 'Dr. Chang', her spirit guide.

J BERNARD HUTTON

Introduced by Dennis Bardens
Epilogue and Medical Glossary by
Dr Michael F Kirkman

LESLIE FREWIN of LONDON

First published 1975 by
Leslie Frewin Publishers Limited,
Five Goodwin's Court,
Saint Martin's Lane,
London WC2N 4LL, England.

Printed in Great Britain by Weatherby Woolnough, Sanders Road,
Wellingborough, Northamptonshire

ISBN 0 85632 125 7

To my wife Pearl and my son Harold
to whom I owe my survival

Contents

INTRODUCTION
by
Dennis Bardens

J Bernard Hutton's detailed and painstaking investigation of
Spiritual Healing is a welcome addition to the growing body
of literature on this puzzling subject.

It is welcome because the incidence of sickness in this country, and
in some others, is growing in simple proportion to the growth of
expenditure on established and orthodox medicine, which has brought
certain old evils under seeming control while proving powerless to cope
with newer, more modern diseases that seem to be inherent in our
complicated industrial society.

It is important, because science, for so long hostile to any sort of
theory or practice that cannot lend itself to standardised and repeatable
results, has refused to acknowledge that there are forces in Nature
defying either definition or explanation within the existing framework
of scientific knowledge – the spectrum of the unexplained intended to
be covered by the broad term 'parapsycholology', or, as some prefer,
'paraphysics'.

Of course, authority entrenched is automatically resentful to any
dimunition, threatened or actual, of its monopolistic powers, an axiom
true of churches, governments, companies, and associations. The
medical profession is no exception to this general rule.

Even so, there is a growing awareness of the existence of potent and
inexplicable forces, including that which, for want of an easier
description, is generally referred to as 'faith, or spiritual, healing'. Yet
the phrase has a certain attractive simplicity. It implies *faith* – of the
healer, who is confident of the power and influences of which he is the

medium; and faith in the sick patient, whose confidence in the healer and his craft embolden him to submit or co-operate as required. *Healing* means the removal of a condition that puts a person below the normal level of health and activity.

Some members of the medical profession, such as Dr Christopher Woodward, are not afraid to say outright that faith healing is a reality. And many universities now have studentships in parapsychology.

Most of us know of people, formerly sick, who truly believe that they regained their health through the ministrations of a faith-healer or a spiritual healer, and if they feel well and happy, and pursue their former healthy lives with their accustomed verve and zest, who is to gainsay them? Perhaps the secret lies in the psychosomatic nature of so much illness and disability; patients lucky enough to find a healer, who has time and patience and love, may commence their cures with that receptivity that comes of sheer trust and confidence.

Furthermore, faith-healers and spiritual healers eschew drugs and medicaments and surgery. Perhaps, as a result, some patients are denied the benefits, such as they are, that might have accrued from such things in their particular case; but if they were denied the supposed benefits, they also avoided the very real hazards. Britain's 23,000 general practitioners are grossly overworked and have simply not the time to give what many a case really requires. Drugs frequently have evil side effects that are discovered too late. The pressure on hospitals is appalling and the standard of treatment uneven. The casualty departments are frequently understaffed, or staffed with semi-trained people whose shortcomings have been ignored because of the difficulty of finding staff, or else they have exaggerated their qualifications. I am thinking of a patient who, after a road accident, was merely treated for a cut forehead when he had, in fact, sustained ten fractured ribs, a fractured collar bone, and a punctured lung. An inquest on a friend of mine who had been receiving deep-ray treatment for cancer revealed, according to a distinguished pathologist, that he did not have cancer at all. Another friend of mine, and a member of the Royal Society of Medicine, suffered bad injuries and lacerations after being knocked down by a hit-and-run car. Twelve days elapsed before the hospital discovered that he had sustained a broken neck!

It is clear that, if faith-healing or spiritual healing is a fact, it can relieve pressure on the existing medical services and relieve the patient from the hazards of more drastic, if more orthodox, treatment.

But is the choice as simple as that?

By what criterion is the patient to know whether the 'spiritual healer' is a person of good character and genuine attainments?

Nobody wishes to see reason dethroned by sheer superstition. Not all patients are people of discernment and sound judgment and, even if they normally are, the discomfort and perhaps fear of the maladies from which they suffer can have impaired their usual judgment. It is a lamentable fact that, amongst the dedicated and sincere healers whose records of achievement would probably compare favourable with those of orthodox doctors, there is intermixed a considerable number of charlatans or people with dangerously nonsensical ideas whose very belief in their alleged special powers makes them more of a social nuisance than they would otherwise be. There are certain conditions which, if not treated appropriately and promptly, will inevitably get worse, either blighting the sufferer's life irretrievably or even proving fatal.

Clearly, recommendation from some known and trusted source is essential to an introduction. And a patient needs to ask himself: how do I *know* that my condition is such-and-such? How, indeed, can one be sure of the healer's diagnoses? What dependable and acceptable records are kept to indicate positive improvement? At what point is it accepted that the patient is 'healed'?

J Bernard Hutton tackles these thorny problems with his customary frankness. We see that while he accepts that cures were effected in some cases, he has reservations about others – that while he himself benefited to some degree, spiritual healing was less effective in the case of his wife and, finally, completely inefficient in his own.

Despite all these necessary warnings, however, the whole field of faith-healing and spiritual healing deserves respectful and thorough study. Mr Hutton has gone to considerable trouble to ascertain and adduce the facts, and to give all sides of the question so that the reader may form his own conclusions. There are few books of this kind with this amount of detail, and, if some readers find the recitation of ills and woes a little hard to bear, they should remember that the sort of breathless (though very readable) survey achieved by the late Godfrey Winn nearly two decades ago is too superficial a basis on which to form a considered judgment.

My own recommendation, for what it is worth, is that some type of supervision or registration may be necessary in this rapidly-expanding field of faith-healing and spiritual healing. It is all too easy for the dotty, the self-deluded, and the rapacious to mislead or exploit those who, often credulous even when in full health, are even more vulnerable in sickness. They need some measure of protection which is at present lacking. Such thoughts ought not to blind us to the immense value that may lie in healing powers that make less pleasant, if not actually dangerous, methods of treatment, unnecessary.

I hope Mr Hutton's book will be widely read and widely discussed.

DENNIS BARDENS

PROLOGUE:

Spiritual Healing

===

C AN THE SICK be healed by means other than medicine or surgery?

The human body is a flesh-and-blood machine. Doctors examine the human machine scientifically, as car mechanics study engines. When a car won't start, the engineer runs a series of tests to trace the cause of the trouble, and then rectifies it. Doctors diagnose the cause of an unhealthy body and prescribe medicines or surgery which will make the human machine work healthily again.

Are *only doctors* able to cure an illness? Are their methods the *only* means to heal the sick?

Throughout history countless healings have been brought about by people who were *not* doctors. The best known healer of all times was Jesus Christ. He is said to have given sight to the blind, cured the sick, and raised the dead. His healings, and others like them, have been called miracles; a miracle being an event which is not understood by human beings. To a primitive man the switching on of a spotlight would be a miracle; he would not be able to understand how a large, bright light could be instantaneously spread over a large area.

Miracles of healing have been demonstrated by many. The Apostles and their successors were notable healers, and Martin Luther cured the sick. Every century since Christ records miraculous cures performed by Baptists, Quakers or Puritans, Methodists, Mormons or Irvingites. Prince Shillinghurst was a great healer and Valentine Greatrakes was known far and wide in the seventeenth century as 'The Stroker', because of his healing method. Hundreds, if not thousands, of healers have been at work throughout the centuries, their names forgotten and their work only occasionally recorded.

Were they truly healers? History records much that can be doubted, and a great deal can be refuted. The miracles of healing performed by Jesus Christ cannot be proved to have taken place; and the miracles of Lourdes are not convincing to the sceptical.

The Roman Catholic Church is extremely reluctant to declare that a miracle has occurred. It first examines all evidence with sceptical zeal. Should any event that the Roman Catholic Church declares a miracle be subsequently proved to have had a natural cause, it would weaken faith in the Church. But whenever the Roman Catholic Church *does* declare a miracle, it attributes it to 'The Power of God'. Even so, it does not follow that a declared miracle may have come about by some cause found to be in accordance with the laws of nature. The primitive man, blinded by a powerful spotlight, may well cry: 'Miracle!' But by increasing his knowledge he will learn that the spotlight functions in accordance with the laws of nature.

Man ceaselessly pursues knowledge; and learning to heal the sick is a worthy objective. But in his study of healing, man may have become lost, and wandered off the highway into the back streets.

Is the only method of curing illness by administering medicines, or by using surgery?

The winds blew over the earth before man existed. They still blew while man fashioned boats and learned to paddle them. But when man, realising that a natural element could be harnessed, made sails, his history was revolutionised. Great oceans were crossed; great discoveries were made; the East met the West and the peoples of the World were drawn together.

For centuries man had laboriously paddled boats while the wind's potentialities were unsuspected and unexploited.

For centuries man has healed the sick with medicines and surgery while persistent claims are made that *there are other methods*. When the winds blew upon the cheeks of the galley-slaves at their oars, spiritual healers were even then easing the suffering of the sick.

Can man's way of healing be improved if spiritual healing is studied scientifically?

When man relied upon the horse, the idea that ordinary water could be converted into a far more powerful means of transport simply by being heated, would have been scoffed at. But a thoughtful man who bothered to ponder upon the steam jetting from the spout of a kettle invented the steam-engine. It is *not* a miracle that water can drive a train. But the natural law governing water must be studied and adapted before it will do so.

The discovery of anaesthetic was a great boon to mankind. It eased suffering and enabled surgeons to operate efficiently. Pain-killing drugs are a priceless boon to those who have need of them. But are drugs and anaesthetic the only way to kill pain?

Hypnosis makes *no* use of drugs or anaesthetic. But surgeons discovered that hypnotised patients feel no pain when operated upon *without* anaesthetic. A patient suffering pain can be relieved of it by hypnotic suggestion.

Doctors acknowledge that hypnosis is effective. But how or why it works is not known. Yet, one day man will doubtless understand hypnosis as thoroughly as he now understands how to make a spotlight.

If spiritual healing is effective, it can be more valuable to mankind than hypnosis. And *how* it works is of secondary importance – for the present.

Does spiritual healing cure the sick? If it can, in any way, then we need to study it and take full advantage of its benefits.

But although miracles of healing are recorded throughout history, widespread scepticism exists about spiritual healing. The 'laying on' of hands to cure the sick seems as improbable to the average man as the spotlight to a primitive savage. However, it should be easy to form a clear-cut opinion about spiritual healing in the twentieth century. It either works, or it doesn't. All we have to do is to put it to the test.

But in practice, this proves almost impossible. The modern man has an extremely sceptical attitude. He will believe almost anything that is scientifically proved by experts. But otherwise there is very little that he is willing to take on trust.

A spiritual healer can cure sick people before a large audience. Yet those same eye-witnesses can remain unconvinced that an act of healing has occurred. Some will not believe what they have seen; and they can give sound reasons for their scepticism. They point out that there could be collusion between the spiritual healer and the patient; the patient may not have been as ill as he seemed; or the entire proceedings may have resulted from a mental hysteria to which the spiritual healer and the patient are sympathetically attuned. These are valid arguments.

Something more convincing than a mere spiritual healing demonstration is required.

The sound way to test spiritual healing is under conditions that guarantee that if spiritual healing occurs it does so *without* fraud or misconception. A series of demonstrations will need to be performed before scientists under the experimental conditions that they stipulate. Such a series would show if spiritual healing is possible; if it can heal the sick; or if it is simply a delusion.

The obvious scientists to supervise such a test experiment would be qualified doctors. But here is the snag. Regrettably, the medical profession does not wish to co-operate in such tests.

It has sound reasons. Doctors must protect the public from confidence tricksters, charlatans and bogus healers who would eagerly provide quack cures where legal loopholes permitted. During the past hundred years the medical profession's high standards of morality and conduct have wiped out fraudulent cures, prevented the sale of spurious cure-all medicines, and discredited the charlatans' strange potions and charms. If the medical profession carelessly stated that spiritual healing were possible, a hundred bogus spiritual healers would spring up where now there is only one, all promising the Elixir of Life. The medical profession has a duty to be as cautious about recognising spiritual healing, as the Roman Catholic Church must be about declaring an event a miracle.

But there seems to be no sound reason why the medical profession should not put spiritual healing to the test under strict controls. Useless cure-all medicines have been exposed as quackery, and the public are better off because of the exposure. If sick people fail to undergo essential surgery because they believe a spiritual healer can cure them – when he is unable to do so – isn't it important that patients should understand they are endangering their lives?

On the other hand, if spiritual healing can cure, the healers possess an ability that could be invaluable to mankind. Their abilities should be studied and the knowledge thus gained made available to the entire medical profession. Nevertheless, despite the many efforts made by some spiritual healers to gain the serious co-operation of the medical profession, it has been witheld.

All groups of professional men resist invasion of their field by unqualified amateurs. Britain is renowned for its impartial dispensing of justice. But it is a sad fact that an ordinary man before the Courts is unlikely to obtain true justice unless a professional lawyer represents him. If a man in court is so unwise as to appear without a lawyer, the judge will warn him he has only himself to blame for any miscarriage of justice that may occur.

Doctors and lawyers have converted their professions into monopolies. Only members of the fraternity are allowed to learn the secret rituals and languages. They have formed closed shops with more stringent regulations and restrictive practices than any Trade Union. And, without doubt, many individual doctors would resent the invasion of their profession by non-qualified spiritual healers with the same passion that Trade Union dockers object to the employment of unskilled, non-ticket holding labourers.

Concern for the intricate structure of the medical profession is probably one of the reasons why doctors have avoided conducting a thorough investigation into spiritual healing. A thorny conflict is involved: on the one hand the desires of well-intentioned men to do everything possible to diminish human suffering; on the other the need to maintain the present high standards of medical dignity that it has taken centuries to achieve.

The only concession the medical profession has made to spiritual healing is to consider a few submitted reports about alleged 'cures'; and to reject them for reasons that did not take account of the full facts. The medical profession has never accorded any spiritual healer the privilege of submitting every facet of his claim to scientific test and scrutiny.

When the British Medical Association published its brief report about its investigation of spiritual healing, it stated flatly that it could find no evidence whatsoever that it cured diseases. The submitted reports showed that patients, who had been written off as hopeless cases by members of the medical profession, had later recovered while being treated by a spiritual healer. The BMA report did not regard this as evidence of cures; it concluded that the original diagnosis was faulty.

It seems unlikely that the medical profession will test out spiritual healing under scientific conditions in the near future. But this tremendous obstacle to the pursuit of knowledge is not insurmountable. An increasing number of individual doctors are taking a very keen interest in the subject, and many actively co-operate unofficially with spiritual healers. All doctors take the Hippocratic Oath and are pledged to heal the sick. If a patient improves under the treatment of a spiritual healer they are pleased.

Organised groups of men traditionally resist changes which affect their organisation's structure. Galileo was condemned by the Roman Catholic Church because his assertion that the earth moved around the sun contradicted its teachings. Darwin was ostracised when he stated his theory of evolution; his argument that man descended from the same roots as the monkey conflicted with Protestant beliefs that man originated with Adam and Eve in the Garden of Eden. Resistance to new ideas is so automatic, and emotional that it would be surprising if spiritual healing *was* welcomed and enthusiastically investigated.

Legends tell of a man who discovered the Elixir of Life. He wanted to share his boon with all men and stood in the market-place, offering his bottles of life-giving liquid for a pittance. But those in the market-place were suspicious, and in desperation the well-intentioned man offered his bottles free of charge! This only confirmed the suspicions of the onlookers. They would not accept the Elixir of Life as a gift.

This legend has a modern version. While taking part in a television programme, a man stood in a busy London street offering genuine £1 notes for sale at a penny each. At the end of a long day only one man had risked a penny to buy. The modern spiritual healer also stands in the market-place. He offers his services to everybody. He is willing to do all he can to heal the sick because of his love of mankind. Some spiritual healers ask only for a 'donation'; others charge substantial fees. Their healing is available to all pockets.

This book examines a spiritual healer in action, and tries to answer the question whether there is anything in her claims.

1

A First Healing Session

HOVE IS CLOSE to Brighton, linked to it by the ribbon of houses that are typical of most of England's coast-line. No 47 Goldstone Villas is exactly what its name suggests: a modest middle-class house in a modest, middle-class neighbourhood.

Mrs Leah Doctors proved to be a bustling, cheerful lady who greeted us warmly. Her sociable personality instantly made us feel at home. There was no hint in her manner that she could perform 'miracles', or even suspected she might do so. Only her clinically white coat suggested an association with healing. But its impact was blunted by the bright-red corduroy trousers she wore under it. Chatting sociably, she led us up a short staircase and into her healing-room, a smallish apartment furnished with a doctor's couch, a stool, and a settee. Still chatting, Mrs Doctors asked my wife to lie on the couch, as though inviting her to have a cup of tea.

But once Pearl lay stretched out upon the couch there was a perceptible change in the atmosphere. Leah stood beside my wife, very quiet and serious. For some moments she seemed to be communing within herself. Presently she laid her hands upon Pearl and moved them around exploratively. She wore a pensive expression, as though she was learning more from thought inspiration than she could by mere tactile contact. Then she asked in a matter-of-fact voice: 'What's wrong with you, my dear?'

Pearl told Mrs Doctors the nature of her illness. Leah talked cosily while she laid her hands on Pearl's body. I wondered why this healing medium did not enter into a trance. She probably picked up my thoughts telepathically, because she answered the question in my mind:

'Though I am guided by my spirit control, I do not always go into trance. Whether I do depends upon my guide.'

Then she said her spirit guide was Dr Chang, who was always beside her when she treated patients and used her as his means to transmit his healing powers. All the time she talked, Leah Doctors' hands moved gently over Pearl. She said Dr Chang was channeling his healing powers through her hands. Presently she asked Pearl if she noticed anything.

'I feel something warm touching me inside,' said Pearl, and Leah nodded as though it was exactly what she'd expected.

The healing session lasted some twenty minutes. All the time Leah willingly answered all my questions about her spirit guide, Dr Chang. She told Pearl she hoped the symptoms of her complaint would recede within the next few days. She made no sweeping promises of a swift healing. On the contrary, she said frankly she was quite unable to say yet if her treatment would help Pearl. Pearl asked if she should return for another healing session, to which Leah replied that if there was no improvement in her condition within a few days, she should telephone and fix another appointment for a month's time.

I was neither impressed nor unimpressed by Leah's treatment. The laying on of hands is a healing method adopted by many spiritual healers. I was interested in results, not methods. I didn't expect an instant, 'miraculous' cure. I was a detached observer, noting facts and reserving judgment. If Pearl showed some benefit from the healing treatment, I intended to ask Leah to grant me a consultation.

We were ready to leave. But as Pearl picked up her handbag to pay the healing fee of £2, Leah looked at me in surprise. She said abruptly: 'Don't *you* wish to consult me?'

'Not yet.'

She didn't hear me. 'You're in *urgent* need of healing.' It was a statement.

'Perhaps an appointment after my wife . . . .'

'Since you are here I'll give you treatment now.' She stared at me intently. 'Your eyes are giving you great trouble.'

Once again I wondered if she was telepathic. My eye trouble was constantly on my mind. Not only was my vision bad, but I suffered constant pain, as though my eyes revolved in sandpaper sockets.

Leah moved the chair close to the window and gestured me to sit down. I sat down slowly. I felt duty-bound to tell Leah I had previously received spiritual healing from Dr Lang, and I described his method of 'Spirit Surgery' upon my 'Spirit Body'.

Leah understood all I was telling her.

'Dr Lang uses a different healing method,' she interrupted me with the confidential air of a theatre nurse discussing different surgeons. 'Dr Chang uses healing rays. These rays remove all impurities from the eyes and strengthen them.'

My face showed my scepticism and she added: 'Dr Chang is very successful with eyes. He's cured many serious eye conditions, including glaucoma. He's even helped registered blind people to see.'

This was an astonishing claim. It would shock most people. But Leah was speaking to *me!* I could *not* be sceptical. I had stood upon the threshold of blindness, and a 'Spirit Doctor' had restored my vision. Leah's statement that Dr Chang could help the blind to see was not, to me, an improbable, presposterous claim. It was one that *could* be true.

'Relax and close your eyes.' Leah stood behind me and placed her fingertips upon my eyelids. Her fingers were cool and instantly soothed the hot, gritty soreness. Every few moments she removed her fingers and flicked her hands as though flipping drops of moisture from them. Her cool fingers were a soothing balm. While she worked, we talked about Dr Chang. And when Dr Chang took over and talked to me through Leah, I was not surprised. Dr Lang had spoken to me through George Chapman in the same way.

'That's all the treatment I can give you for the present,' said Dr Chang. 'Your eyes are very weak and can't absorb more strength from the healing rays for the present. Now we'll deal with your other troubles.'

Leah's cool fingers glided up to my forehead.

'I am treating you for head pains now,' said Dr Chang. 'I can look into you and see what's causing your pain. The healing rays will soon put it right.'

Leah's cool fingers left my forehead. I felt a cool air waft upon my cheeks as she flicked her hands, and knew instant relief from pain, as though her cool fingers sucked out from my brain an evil fluid that was poisoning it.

'Almost finished,' said Dr Chang. 'You'll soon feel much better.'

'I feel better already,' I told him. 'The head pains have gone.'

'How about your eyes?'

'They don't burn so much; the soreness has eased. How can I thank you?'

'Don't thank me,' said Dr Chang quietly. 'Thank God. All healing comes from God and His healing power. We're only God's instruments.' He paused a moment and added: 'I'm going now. We'll talk again when you come for your next treatment.'

Leah was motionless for some minutes before she passed out of her trance. At once she was the laughing, bustling, cheerful woman who'd welcomed us to her home. 'Dr Chang has been able to help you a lot,' she told me.

'I can see you a lot more clearly now; and my head pains have vanished,' I confirmed.

'But be sure to visit again next week,' she said as I paid her the £4 fee for Pearl's treatment and mine.

My first meeting with Dr Chang was in June 1972. There were to be many more, and I was to learn much more about him and his methods.

2

A Book
is Born

D URING THE FOLLOWING days there was a steady improvement in my eyesight. Every day my vision was clearer and I could increasingly distinguish objects from a greater distance.

Unhappily, Pearl's condition did *not* change. She believed there was a very slight improvement, but it was virtually imperceptible. But we decided we were being too demanding. Leah Doctors had given us no hope of a swift recovery. Indeed, she'd anticipated that Pearl would need more treatment within a month.

I attended for my next appointment with Dr Chang, and, as soon as I was seated and Leah had placed her fingers upon my eyelids, she went into a trance. Dr Chang spoke to me and said I was responding well to his treatment. He said he'd 'be able to heal my eyes completely. 'Afterwards you'll probably see much better that at any time in your life.' he said. 'You'll be able to work longer hours without the severe eye-strain you've suffered in the past.'

The treatment was as previously. Leah's cool fingers soothed my eyes while she helped Dr Chang direct his healing rays upon me. I grew accustomed to the burning sensation of a hot ray circling slowly around my eyeballs until my eyes were warm from its glow. And while Leah's fingers soothed my eyelids Dr Chang chatted to me with warm friendliness. I told him about my initial scepticism, my visit to Dr Lang, and my conversion to belief in Dr Lang's spiritual healing. I told him I'd written a book about spiritual healing* and the conversation drifted

* *Healing Hands*

to the feasibility of writing a book about Dr Chang's methods.

Spiritual healing is not the monopoly of a few mediums who select their patients, Dr Chang told me when I asked him about payment terms for his treatment. Those who possess healing gifts have a simple duty to heal the sick for a reasonable remuneration. Their healing services are available to everyone. Spiritual healers must not seek fame nor wealth. They are not merchants. They do not sell services or a commodity. A price-tag cannot be placed upon health.

'Spiritual healers do *not* possess special powers,' Dr Chang said. 'They are healing mediums; and healing mediums are simply human instruments through whom doctors in the spirit world can work. Dedicated healing mediums are pleased to be used for a worthy cause and are happy to help ease suffering. But they must live. Like all other human beings they need food, and Leah charges only £2 per patient for a consultation.

'Spiritual healers should not seek publicity to increase their personal image or income,' continued Dr Chang. 'But they do not avoid publicity; because in this sceptical world they are not treating enough patients. They could relieve much more suffering if spiritual healing was better understood.

'There are so many unfortunate people I could help,' said Dr Chang wryly, 'if they learned about spiritual healing and were prompted to seek our help.'

As we talked, ideas for the book took shape in Dr Chang's mind. But I had no intention of becoming a publicity agent for Dr Chang and Leah Doctors. I would be prepared to write about Dr Chang's healing rays, I told him, but I would insist on putting them to the test as far as possible. I said this bluntly and Dr Chang wholeheartedly agreed with me. He pointed out that if I wrote the book while receiving treatment from him I'd be in an ideal position to form a personal judgment about his work.

But I required much more than this, I told him. I wanted his permission and his co-operation in my investigation of his cases. I wanted to know the official medical condition of patients *before* they visited him; and their official medical condition *after* his treatment. I wanted permission to approach his patients and question them.

Dr Chang assured me I'd receive his full co-operation. He could not give me an undertaking that his patients would be willing to be interviewed. But he had no objection to me consulting them.

I said I'd want to interview him also, and ask searching questions. When he agreed to this, I added that I wanted our interviews to be tape-recorded, as our previous and present healing sessions and discussions had been.

'There can be no objection to that,' said Dr Chang. 'I'll answer all your "searching questions", as you call them. I want the book to be accurate and completely truthful.'

'Then when will you be ready to start?'

'Haven't we already started?' Dr Chang asked gently.

He promised me all the help I needed because he wanted the book to be successful. He wanted people everywhere to know that spiritual healing can, and does, cure the sick. He said: *'Those who are ill and suffering must learn that they can be helped through spiritual healing.'*

I'd grown enthusiastic about writing this book, although no such idea had been in my mind when I'd kept this second appointment with Dr Chang. I hurried home with ideas bubbling in my mind and at once sat down and mapped out a rough outline of this book's contents.

I'd been working more than three hours when Pearl called me to dinner. As I stretched myself to ease my cramp after hunching over my desk so long, I realised that not only was I thinking very clearly, but that my eyes hadn't troubled me all the time I was writing.

As far as I personally was concerned, Dr Chang's healing rays seemed to give excellent results.

But what would his other patients report?

3

What is a Healing Medium?

WHAT IS A healing medium? Who is Leah Doctors? What is this mysterious influence that sends mediums into a trance, and converts them into instruments of the 'Spirit World'?

There are few practising healing mediums. But there are probably very many potential mediums.

Throughout time men and women have been 'possessed'. Some have names that have echoed ceaselessly through the centuries. Many have a secure niche in history, like Joan of Arc, who fearlessly obeyed the voices that spoke to her, even though they sent her to a fiery death. In the Middle Ages, thousands of 'possessed' people were tortured and cruelly executed, accused of being 'witches'.

There were so many in those days that a Holy Inquisition was set up to smell them out and destroy them. In our somewhat less barbaric age, 'possessed' people are treated with less viciousness and more tolerance. They are pitied as having 'bats in the belfry', dismissed as 'religious fanatics', or condemned as 'clever tricksters'. But usually, except for their 'queerness' in being 'possessed', they seem good, well-meaning, and quite ordinary people.

Joan of Arc was an *ordinary* peasant girl. She was uneducated and couldn't write. But when she crossed verbal swords with the Inquisitors, who were learned men, she displayed a lucidity of mind and a clarity of speech that exposed them as slaves of dogma and with minds imprisoned.

More recently, Patience Worth has become notable because careful records have been kept about her activities while she was 'possessed'. In 1913, when Mrs Curran first went into a trance and was 'possessed' by the 'spirit' of Patience Worth, men had grown less bigoted about witchcraft and were more inquiring. Mrs Curran was not dismissed as having 'bats in the belfry'. Over a period of fourteen years scientists subjected Mrs Curran to every kind of scientific test, under conditions which *they* imposed and which eliminated all possibility of trickery. Using Mrs Curran as her medium, Patience Worth wrote many books and poems which were widely published. She wrote at enormous speed, one estimate being a hundred words a minute. Scientists were astonished by the language used in the books. The spirit Patience Worth claimed she had lived in 1670, and the books which Mrs Curran wrote were in the language of that period. Many of the words and phrases had dropped out of use, but the professors who researched seventeenth-century speech subsequently investigated and were able to confirm that Mrs Curran used the authentic language of that period.

What could Mrs Curran, an ordinary housewife, have known of seventeenth-century English that the academics didn't know until they looked it up?

Many mediums are ordinary women. Who is Leah Doctors?

Leah's father was a Rumanian named Wasserman who was brought to England at the age of twelve. Leah's mother was Russian and she also emigrated to England when she was twelve. Leah was born in Essex in September 1913. Her early childhood was happy and secure; her parents owned a furriers' business and two drapers' shops. But the slump after the First World War, and the dishonesty of a business associate, brought ruin to the Wasserman family. Thus, at the age of ten, Leah found herself in London's Whitechapel Road, attending Commercial Street School and with poverty as the keynote of her schooldays. Often the meagre rent couldn't be paid and as often there were hungry mouths. Leah was only one of six children and the Wasserman's economic struggle was grim. It eased only when the children reached school-leaving age and could go out to work. Leah was apprenticed to a dressmaker when she was fourteen, and eventually became a furrier. Her humdrum working life was no different from that of other working people.

But Leah was not quite like other people. She was 'possessed'. She discovered this when she was eight years of age and learning to play the piano. Every evening she practised in the parlour which was lit by gas and Leah practised by candle-light. In this room at a tender age she learned that she could be 'possessed'. She related the incident into my tape-recorder:

> After I'd finished practising one day, I looked at the huge painting of Queen Victoria which covered one wall from ceiling to floor. I saw her eyes become alive and look out at me. In that moment she seemed to come out of the picture towards me. I was frightened and ran out of the room to my mother. I told her: 'Mum, Queen Victoria is after me! She's come out of the picture!' Mother laughed and led me back to the parlour. 'Look,' she said, 'Queen Victoria is still in the picture.' But she couldn't see what I saw. I could see the painting, but I could also see the Queen standing apart from the picture. It was so clear I was insistent: 'Can't you see her, Mum? The picture's there; but she's *here!*' But mother couldn't be convinced. And it was then I realised I was seeing something Mum couldn't see. Many years later I realised that by concentrating upon Queen Victoria I must have drawn her spirit into the room. But I was a child then and couldn't understand this. But I did know the vision didn't intend me any harm and I wasn't afraid. I've *never* been afraid of spirits.

Leah possessed her healing gift at the age of eight but didn't know it. Her father loved animals and she learned to love them too. Neighbouring children brought their sick pets to her and when she cuddled and stroked them they got better. If an animal met with an accident or had a bone stuck in its throat, she would be called upon to comfort it and help the healing process.

But it was not until she was in her teens that Leah discovered accidentally that she possessed healing powers. Her younger sister came home from work with her head and eyes aching. Leah stroked her forehead and rested her fingers upon her sister's eyes. 'Your hands are so cool,' commented her sister, and a little while later added: 'My eyes are quite better. They feel like velvet. The headache has gone.'

Leah and her brothers and sisters, like many people, had tried to make contact with the 'spirit world'. They'd played the ever-popular Ouijah game of placing an upturned tumbler upon the table, resting their fingertips upon it, and watching it slide round within a circle of letters. It was not a serious attempt to communicate with the spirit world; but Leah later realised they received many messages which foretold the future. She cited one example when I asked for it: her brother was told he would visit Egypt, which at the time seemed most improbable; but, when war broke out two years later, Leah's brother was posted to Egypt.

During the Second World War, Leah's family moved from White-chapel to Stamford Hill, London. Leah, meanwhile, became increasingly interested in Spiritualism, attended seances and received training to be a direct voice medium. While training, she went into a trance and was possessed by a spirit guide who said his name was White Feather. When he spoke through Leah, his deep voice reverberated around the room. Leah then discovered she could enter into a semi-trance – a curious state that enabled her to ask her spirit guide questions that he answered; as though she was having a conversation with herself.

Leah's mother allowed a social club to hold its weekly meetings in her house. At one of these meetings Leah was introduced to Jack Doctors. They were subsequently married at Hackney Town Hall in October 1939. Leah was tailoring and the newly-married couple first lived in furnished rooms, but eventually moved to an unfurnished flat in Bethune Road, Clapton.

The war had made life in London very difficult and Leah, who was weary of moving around, asked White Feather when she would be able to settle down. She sighed with relief when he told her that she'd live in Bethune Road for many years. Having established the nest, Leah's next question was natural for a woman: 'How many children will I have?' White Feather told her she'd have one child: a boy. He was born a year later.

Jack Doctors' parents came from Russia in 1905, and he was born in Bethnal Green in December 1912. Later the family moved to Chingford, and at the age of seventeen Jack was a physical culture enthusiast and studied osteopathy. He passed examinations at the Kilburn Foot Hospital, became a State Registered Chiropodist, and later qualified as an Osteopath.

While her son was an infant, Leah devoted her life to caring for her son, her husband, and her home. But when the boy was old enough to permit it, Leah went out to work again. Like most other married couples who went out to work, Leah and Jack shared the household chores and happily watched their son grow.

It wasn't until 1955, when Leah was forty-two years of age, that she was shunted on to the spiritual healing path. She was employed in a small tailoring business and its proprietor, Mr Soskin, worked as hard as, if not harder than, his staff. He was a cutter and stooped over his work-bench, wielding busy scissors, for long hours every day. Leah noticed one day as he straightened up to ease his aching back that he grimaced with pain. Impulsively Leah sympathised with him and he told her that his backache was getting steadily worse. He'd been taking pills for two years but they were losing their power to give him ease. Compassionately, Leah overcame her concern about being considered odd, and suggested that she should give him spiritual healing treatment. Mr Soskin, who'd tried everything else and had nothing to lose, agreed without enthusiasm.

Twice a day then, during the morning and afternoon tea-breaks, Leah gave her employer treatment. The results were encouraging. At the end of the week Mr Soskin was delighted. His pain had vanished and he could stoop or stand straight with ease. He was so impressed that he praised Leah's healing gift to other employees and they too began to come to Leah with all their little aches and pains. Within her own circle she gained the reputation of possessing healing powers.

It was soon after this that Leah's life was completely transformed. She was at home not thinking of anything in particular — an unguarded moment. Abruptly, Leah felt herself possessed by a spirit, a feeling to which she was accustomed, having been often possessed by White Feather. She knew instantly that this spirit was a kind and loving soul; she felt warmed by his radiant happiness and serenity. The spirit informed Leah he wished her to be his medium and help him relieve suffering. He said he could heal through Leah and had the power to cure many types of illness. The spirit made a startling request, one which would put any spiritual healer severely to the test. He asked Leah to find a hunchback; together they would heal him.

Leah had received the call. She longed to respond to it. She was ready to be a healing medium if she could help alleviate pain. But how was she to go about it? She couldn't grab people off the streets and ask them if they wanted to be healed. And it was useless to offer her services to a hospital without possessing even the most minor qualifications.

Leah eventually enrolled at Phil Wyndham's Spiritual Healing Centre, which was close to Amhurst Road in Stoke Newington, above Salter's Cafe. Phil Wyndham had united some half dozen spiritual healers who met at the Centre once a week to receive and treat patients. Leah was welcomed into the group and began healing as a trance-medium. She was guided by the new spirit whom she now knew as Dr Chang.

'I displayed an unusual talent for diagnosis,' Leah stated. 'As soon as

I was entranced, and often before I even went into a trance, I could state the nature of a patient's illness. The other healers in the group hadn't my ability to diagnose and Wyndham organised the healing sessions so that I could devote myself exclusively to diagnosing illnesses. The patients were then passed on to those healers in the group who were most dedicated to treat the illness.'

Swift and correct diagnosis was valuable to the healing group. But Dr Chang and Leah were not making the best use of their healing powers. Leah tried to find time for direct healing, but the demand upon her as a diagnostician grew heavier. Moreover, the group met only once a week.

Leah finally realised that she could do healing work adequately only if she had her own centre and worked full time. Dr Chang insisted that he had the power to heal even the most serious illnesses. But he couldn't heal if he had no patients. He said he could remove tumours on the brain and heal serious head injuries; mend broken bones swiftly and cure diseases of the eyes, including glaucoma; alleviate deafness, bronchitis and heart complaints; and heal spinal injuries. But Dr Chang's power was wasted if Leah couldn't put it to use.

The Doctors were not wealthy. They lived comfortably because Leah and her husband both worked. To give up her safe job, abandon her present way of life and devote herself to spiritual healing full time involved personal risk and economic sacrifice. But neither Leah nor Jack was discouraged by personal considerations. In consultation with Dr Chang, Leah decided to launch her own spiritual healing sanctuary.

4

Doctors are Astounded

LEAH DOCTORS HAD no wealthy patron to pay the rent for suitable premises. Instead, she converted her home in Bethune Road into a spiritual healing sanctuary.

Her first patient was Mrs Betty Usher who had recently moved into the downstairs flat. Mrs Usher was completely blind. She made her way around her flat by groping with her hands. She was also a diabetic.

Mrs Usher had only a vague notion of what spiritual healing was about when Leah compassionately suggested she should give her treatment. Mrs Usher climbed the stairs to Leah's flat with the patient air of a neighbour willing to do her best to be sociable.

What happened in Leah's small room could be described as a 'miracle' if the event had taken place under approved conditions set up by investigating scientists. Leah placed her hands upon Mrs Usher's eyelids – as she had done upon mine – and sank into a trance. Dr Chang then directed his healing rays upon Mrs Usher, and when Leah removed her fingers half-an-hour later, Mrs Usher could *SEE!*

Even Leah, who had faith in her spirit guide as all mediums must, was stunned with joy; ever afterwards she has shared Mrs Usher's joy that she can see again. But Dr Chang wasn't yet finished with Mrs Usher. She needed a series of healing sessions, he said, to get rid of the diabetes.

The human body is an engine of flesh and blood, and the fuel that drives it is food and liquid. Diabetic people's bodies cannot adequately break down and absorb the sugar in their system. Sugar is an essential fuel; but if the body does not absorb it properly, the blood is dangerously overloaded with sugar. The great danger all diabetics face is that they may unknowingly drift into a coma. They are then unable to inject themselves with insulin which helps break down the excess of sugar in their bloodstream.

Mrs Usher was under the care of the hospital in Whitechapel where the doctors had recommended her an intake of eighty units of insulin. This dosage was not a cure, however, for her illness; no cure for diabetes has yet been found. Mrs Usher's daily intake of insulin was merely to help her to live a normal life and to keep at bay the ever-present danger of coma.

Mrs Usher was treated by Leah once a week for three months. At the end of the treatment Mrs Usher returned to the hospital for examination. Her doctors were astounded; she was completely free of diabetes. It was inexplicable. They said Mrs Usher was unique, and she was invited to attend a special meeting at which her case was to be discussed.

Mrs Usher quietly explained to the doctors how she'd felt herself getting steadily better week by week, while she received Leah Doctors' spiritual healing treatment. Some doctors frowned, some grinned; some looked angry, others were thoughtful. But whatever they thought about Mrs Usher's explanation, one stark fact still stood out clearly: Mrs Usher had been suffering from diabetes. Now she wasn't!

One doctor put forward a possible explanation. He pointed out that Mrs Usher's rather high intake of eighty units of insulin may have had the effect of giving an insulin shock to her metabolism, and this shock had set it working properly again. But Mrs Usher destroyed this unlikely theory. She revealed that soon after Leah Doctors began her healing treatment she'd felt a distinct improvement in herself. She'd tested her urine first thing every morning, and, entirely upon her own initiative, she'd steadily reduced her daily intake of insulin. Long before Leah's treatment was finished, she'd ceased to take insulin.

The doctors could find no scientific explanation of Mrs Usher's cure. One doctor said wryly that if Mrs Usher had a relapse, a recurrence of her disease, she'd be well advised to contact Leah Doctors again because *they* couldn't cure her; they could only prescribe insulin to keep her diabetes in check.

When these words are being written in 1972, seventeen years have elapsed since Dr Chang healed Mrs Usher. Today, she is in the best of health. She never diets, eats what she fancies, has not suffered a recurrence of diabetes, and has not used insulin again. She can also thread a needle and cotton with ease.

Mrs Betty Usher was the first great cure of Dr Chang and Leah Doctors. The success inspired Leah. She now knew that diabetes could be cured; she'd be able to heal other diabetics. She was also given encouragement by a member of the medical profession. She received a letter from a Harley Street consultant* who was dedicated to his profession and made frequent visits to America to keep abreast of medical knowledge.

This physician was a genuine seeker after the truth. He'd heard that diabetes had been cured, and he wanted to know how it had been done. At his invitation Leah called upon him at his consulting-room and they talked for a long time. But Leah could give him little practical help. She told him she was an instrument through which Dr Chang worked; she told him about Dr Chang's healing rays; and explained that, as her diabetic patients felt their condition improve, they gradually cut down their insulin intake.

Regrettably, there was no common basis from which Leah and the consultant could work in co-operation. He told her she had a wonderful gift. He was a specialist but was quite unable to cure diabetes. Since Leah had enjoyed such excellent results, he urged her to devote herself to healing diabetes, because nobody else could.

This was a sound suggestion and Leah tried to follow it. But she soon discovered she was the man in the market-place offering wares that were suspect. She had only a few diabetic patients but she could handle many more. It seemed logical to Leah she should offer her services where they could do most good. Accordingly, she proposed to the British Diabetic Association that they send her some of their members as patients for treatment. The patient's precise medical condition could be controlled by the Association, and any improvement or otherwise could be noted and investigated.

This proposition, if accepted, would have provided an excellent opportunity to test and assess Leah's claim of being able to cure diabetes. But, unhappily, Leah's offer was declined: 'It is indeed kind of you to offer your services to our members, but I am afraid that this is an entirely individual matter for diabetics and not for the Diabetic Association.'

* Due to medical etiquette, the identity of this Harley Street Physician cannot be revealed.

This lack of co-operation dissolved Leah's hopes of specialising in healing diabetes, the illness in which she'd discovered she possessed an unusual healing gift. Instead, she began to practice her healing powers upon all who suffered, no matter what their ailments.

Little by little Dr Chang's and Leah's healing achievements became better known, as grateful patients talked about their cures. The psychic magazines took an interest and published accounts of some of Leah's most notable successes. Even local and national newspapers reported her healings when the circumstances were 'newsy' enough. Leah received letters from all over the United Kingdom, from America, and many other parts of the world. She gave 'absent healing' to sufferers and was able to devote herself full-time to healing the sick.

But before this happy stage was reached, Leah suffered many setbacks. There were many obstacles she had to fight and overcome.

5

Public Demonstrations

AFTER MONTHS OF spiritual healing at Bethune Road, Leah was happy with her success but sadly disappointed that she had few patients. She treated an average of twenty a week, but she was healthy and energetic and able to heal many more. Whenever she heard about, or saw, people who suffered from incurable diseases, she felt frustrated. She believed that if they consulted her, she could help them. But before the sick could visit Leah, they had to know that she was available for consultation. Leah and Jack Doctors considered ways to inform the public that spiritual healing might be worth trying out.

It was a bigger problem than they'd realised. They approached the Press first, but, although journalists were ready to splash spiritual healing if it had a newsworthy twist, they were unwilling to become Leah's publicity agent; or to recommend sick people to visit her. It is against the policy of the Press to give such publicity; and qualified doctors, or pharmaceutical laboratories, would have fared no better than Leah.

Leah and Jack Doctors had already failed to obtain co-operation from the British Diabetic Association, but, undeterred, they approached doctors and hospitals, and offered Leah's services. These offers were often declined regretfully. Doctors and hospital staff have to abide by General Medical Council rules, and these state flatly that medical practitioners on the GMC Register *cannot* collaborate with unregistered practitioners.

Jack admitted defeat. He concluded they were banging their heads against granite-hard barriers; they couldn't break down time-honoured rules and regulations. But Leah wouldn't be discouraged. She thought it insane that ill people should be deprived of the opportunity to know about spiritual healing because of man-made laws. And as though to strengthen her resolution, she was visited by an unusual patient.

Anne Winne lived in Stamford Hill, not far from Leah. She'd heard about Leah's healing sanctuary by pure chance. She visited Leah at once because she had nothing to lose. Anne was willing to try anything, for she suffered from kyphosis. She was under medical care but doctors had told her she could never become normal. She was doomed to live the rest of her life with a hump on her back. It was caused by a spinal deformity that compressed her rib cage and seriously impaired her breathing.

One of Dr Chang's very first suggestions to Leah had been that she should bring a hunchback to heal. Now she had one! Anne Winne had borne her hunch for eight years; she was a most deserving case for Dr Chang's healing rays.

Anne visited Leah for three healing sessions. Afterwards this is what she reported:

> After three treatments my spine was perfectly straight, my hump was gone and I felt much stronger. Mrs Doctors placed her hands upon my back and I felt a warm glow flow through my body. It was like an electric current that lasted about ten minutes during the course of each visit.
>
> With each healing session my back became straighter and my breathing easier. What I thought impossible, has happened! Despite all that the doctors said, I am cured! It's wonderful to be able to stand straight, and walk again. I now feel years younger.

Leah wondered how many hunchbacks and diabetics would leap at the opportunity to undergo spiritual healing if they knew what it could do for them. Leah and Jack discussed ways and means of reaching out to such people and toyed with the idea of giving a public demonstration of spiritual healing. They decided to put it into practice after Dr Chang had approved the plan.

Once again Leah had to face a financial crisis. Money was needed to hire a hall and to publicise the meeting. Leah and Jack broke into their meagre savings and booked the Alliance Hall in Westminster. They printed leaflets and advertised their healing demonstration as widely as their funds permitted.

THE HEALING POWER

Leah's first public demonstration of spiritual healing took place on the 3rd September 1957. To her delight, people flocked into the hall long before the advertised time. When the demonstration began every seat was occupied and people crowded the aisles and lined the stage. Leah started the meeting with a simple prayer for health and peace. Jack explained that he and Leah would work simultaneously on either side of the stage; he would give osteopathic treatment, and Dr Chang would give spiritual healing treatment through Leah. Those in need of healing were invited to come up on the stage.

Leah's first patient was Eileen Cole, from Kilburn, London. She was under the care of the Western Ophthalmic Hospital. Her medical record card stated that her eyesight was severely restricted by an advanced cataract. She had almost no vision and had to be tuided up on to the platform. Leah gave Eileen healing treatment for only a few minutes. When she removed her fingers from Eileen's eyelids, the girl opened her eyes, looked around, and shouted: 'I can see! I can see!' She was so overjoyed she wanted everyone present to know she was healed and demonstrated it by reading aloud advertising print at some distance from her.

Leah was giving a public demonstration of healing in order to prove that she could heal. But she had not invited a group of objective scientific observers to study her at work. Any member of the audience could have assumed that her healing demonstration was a fraud, and that Eileen Cole was a hired stooge. Yet any interested sceptic could also have accompanied Eileen Cole later to the Western Ophthalmic Hospital for her regular check-up. They could have witnessed the ophthalmic surgeon's astonishment, and his statement that Eileen's instantaneous recovery of sight was clinically impossible!

Among the audience that night was Miss Evadne Price, a feature writer, who'd been provided with a chair on the platform. Miss Price realised that if what she had witnessed was genuine, it was beyond the understanding of man, and could rank as a 'miracle'. When miracles are performed they should arouse awe and wonderment. But people often do not realise the significance of what they have witnessed, and Evadne Price later wrote about this audience reaction:*

> It was all so matter-of-fact, so devoid of effect, that nobody realised at first how remarkable it all was. It was like pouring champagne into a pewter pot. There was no sparkle.

* *Two Worlds,* Sept. 14, 1957

Suddenly came one of the most dramatic moments I have ever known. In my journalistic capacity I have interviewed most of the big noises in the psychic world and I have seen some hair-raising things. But nothing has ever eclipsed the instantaneous cure of Hilda Hewitt, of Fulham. You can repeat 'instantaneous'.

Miss Hewitt, a week out of hospital for nerves of the back, was due in again within a few days for an operation. She was in such pain when she sat down that she wished she hadn't come up for treatment, she told me afterwards. She cringed when Mr Doctors touched her neck.

'She's got arthritis of the spine,' said Leah.

'The hospital says it's nerves of the back,' the patient replied.

'No, arthritis, I can feel the great lump here.' I saw Mr Doctors run his hand along the young woman's spine and press. She gave a startled cry . . . and slumped, flat out. At the same moment the healer fell back against the wall as though he had been shot.

I have never been so frightened. I thought the Healer had killed her. I yelled: 'Water.' I caught Miss Hewitt and propped her up. The audience stood up, craning their necks, you could have heard a pin drop . . .

'Here's the water.'

'I don't want water.' Hilda Hewitt shook her head and stood up. 'I'm cured. There was an electric shock and the pain went, and it was so sudden I nearly passed out.' She swept me aside and addressed the audience: 'I'm cured – I've had all these months of agony, and he's cured me.'

The audience began to cheer. I sat back, getting my second wind. I watched Mr Doctors stagger back. He flopped on the steps beside my chair. 'What happened – will someone tell me?' I whispered.

'It was like an electric shock – she got it and so did I. It was like being struck by lightning. I've never had such an experience,' said Mr Doctors. 'I'll never forget it.'

It certainly was a moment to remember.

But I'm a reporter, a bit sceptical, and only satisfied with facts. Did those two know each other? Was all this a put-up job? I asked Miss Hewitt bluntly how long she had known the Doctors family?

She'd never seen Mr Doctors before, she assured me. She had, a few nights earlier, been told at a public demonstration of clairvoyance by Joseph Benjamin that she would not go back into hospital on the 10th, she would be healed in the interval. Seeing this healing meeting advertised, she had come. It was as simple as that.

If Evadne Price had accompanied Miss Hewitt to hospital at the appointed date, she would have witnessed how, after an examination, she was informed that an operation was no longer necessary. She was in good health. And fifteen years later, Mrs Doctors confirmed that Miss Hewitt was still in good health and said she had never had a repetition of her back trouble.

If scientific investigators had been present that night they would have taken note of another unusual phenomenon. 'When the healing shock passed through me, the hands of my watch buckled and my watch stopped at a quarter to nine, the precise instant of my cure.' Miss Hewitt reported. It was a small gold watch on a thin gold bracelet. It has been examined by many people and its hands are still bent, telling the time at 8.45. Miss Hewitt has never had the watch repaired and keeps it in memory of what she calls 'the most wonderful moment in my life,' the moment when she was transformed from a very sick woman into a healthy one.

Miss Hewitt's cure was startling for yet another reason. Jack Doctors was an osteopath, not a medium. But he believed he was helped by the spirit world. What happened to him and Hilda Hewitt surprised both of them equally. Jack Doctors told me:

'When one is stunned with a powerful electric shock that knocks you back – and that's what happened when Hilda Hewitt was on the platform at the Alliance Hall – one must accept that there is a higher power, even if one can't understand it or figure it out. And this electric shock was not hypnosis, or imagination; it was a powerful external force.'

The audience that night in the Alliance Hall was privileged to see many remarkable cures.

Mrs Bentley of Earl's Court, fifty-seven years of age, had been stone deaf in her left ear since the age of seven. The deafness was said to have been caused after a bout of bronchitis. She frequently consulted specialists and hospitals, hoping her hearing would be restored. She was always told that neither medical treatment nor surgery could restore her hearing. Leah Doctors placed her hands upon Mrs Bentley's ears for three or four minutes. Mrs Bentley reported a kind of burning in her head, as though something inside it was being moved around. Then Leah removed her hands and spoke quietly into Mrs Bentley's left ear. Mrs Bentley was astonished. 'I can hear!' she said. 'After being stone deaf in this ear I can hear again!'

Evadne Price requested permission to make a test. She covered Mrs Bentley's good ear and whispered a question softly into the other ear. Mrs Bentley clearly heard the question and answered it. A nose, throat and ear specialist later confirmed that Mrs Bentley's hearing was quite normal. She has had no recurrence of deafness.

A queue of sick people waited their turn to climb on to the platform; Leah and Jack healed many that night of migraine, bronchitis, failing vision, and other illnesses. Leah and Jack Doctors gave of themselves freely, and were tired but content. They had relieved a great deal of suffering by the time the meeting ended.

But there was a wry sequel. A collection was made, and when the pennies and silver coins were totalled, Leah and Jack did not have enough to cover their expenses. But they were not downhearted. They'd been able to help many sick people and this more than compensated them for being out of pocket. They were so satisfied with their evening's work that they booked the Alliance Hall again for two weeks later.

On 17th September 1957, Leah and Jack Doctors gave a second public demonstration of healing. Again, Leah began with a short prayer for health and peace, and told the audience that Dr Chang, her spirit guide, used healing rays to effect his cures.

That night, many of the sick people who had been cured at Leah's first public demonstration, had asked if they could demonstrate they were benefiting from their healing. So for a short time these grateful people gave testimony to Leah's healing gift. Then Leah and Jack again invited those in need of healing to come to the platform.

Mrs Metz of Hendon limped on to the stage. Her left foot was completely rigid, its bones calloused together through arthritis. For two years she'd been unable to move her toes. Medical consultants could do nothing for her except prescribe drugs to ease her pain. Jack Doctors used a combination of osteopathic and spiritual healing and within a few minutes Mrs Metz was wriggling her toes and watching them in amazement. She no longer felt pain. Fifteen years later Leah Doctors confirmed that Mrs Metz reported she is still quite free from arthritic pains.

Mrs MacCarthy was also treated by Jack Doctors. She endured continuous pain resulting from a spinal disease. She had attended a hospital in Cardiff for some years but the doctors could do nothing to heal her. She was so desperate she'd travelled from Cardiff to London solely to attend the meeting. Jack Doctors' combination of osteopathic and spiritual healing relieved her of pain within minutes. Overjoyed, she told the audience she had been cured. But Jack contradicted her: she needed more treatment to prevent a relapse. Mrs MacCarthy made the long journey from Cardiff to London four times subsequently. It was well worth while, Jack Doctors stated proudly and added: As a result she found herself permanently cured of her illness.

Evadne Price was once again upon the platform and described for her readers the healing of a Mrs Fletcher:*

First, he (Dr Chang) invited me to feel the lump in the patient's abdomen. It was like a hard ball, and I felt a bit sick. I then stood back and watched a spirit operation performed, which I have never seen before.

The medium's hands didn't seem to touch Mrs Fletcher at all, just hover. Then Chang's voice said, 'You will go home after and drink much cold water to clear the poison.' The spirit voice then asked me to feel the lump again. It was dispersed.

I assure you the hard ball had gone. I felt slightly dazed...

I have since learned that Mrs Fletcher had an internal growth. Her doctor located it and referred her to hospital for examination by a specialist. The consultant confirmed the doctor's diagnosis, and arrangements were made for her to enter hospital to undergo a surgical operation. Mrs Fletcher was dreading the operation. Her apprehension was so great that she attended the Alliance Hall healing demonstration in the desperate hope that she might escape the surgeon's knife. When she attended the hospital again after Leah's healing treatment, a pre-operational examination showed that the growth scheduled to be surgically removed no longer existed. Mrs Fletcher was discharged from hospital after being warned that if the growth reappeared she must report to hospital again. In the Autumn of 1972, when I enquired about Mrs Fletcher, I learned she had had no recurrence of the growth which Dr Chang had dispersed in September 1957.

* *Two Worlds*, Sept 28, 1957

Many people were healed that night. But not all healings are spectacular. Often a patient's illness is not visually in evidence.

Therefore, the healing influence is not immediately apparent. Some serious illnesses often required many healing sessions. And there are, too, quite a few patients whom Dr Chang cannot cure or even help.

Mrs Carmen Wheeler of New York happened to be in London and attended the Alliance Hall demonstration. She needed spiritual healing and told Leah there were only simple things wrong with her, but that it wasn't very nice to have them a long time. She suffered permanent fatigue and intermittent pains in her arms and back. After treatment by Dr Chang she told Leah she felt very much better and free of pain.

Equally undramatic was the healing of Mrs Wheeler's daughter who suffered attacks of amnesia. She was treated by Leah, and after subsequent healing sessions she eventually ceased to suffer any attacks.

Once again the expense of public healing had to be borne mainly by Leah and Jack Doctors. But again they were content. They had healed people who might never have known they could benefit from spiritual healing, and the knowledge that it was efficacious was spreading widely.

6

'Spirit Doctors' In The 'Spirit World'

IN THE FIFTEENTH century, daring men in fragile ships braved vast oceans while wise men and thinkers pondered if the world was as flat as it looked. Adventurous men, spurred by greed of wealth to be earned by trading, drove their slave-galleys and their square-sailed ships furiously, constantly searching for rich prizes. The coastal vessels that plied the Mediterranean from Greece to Spain, then north to Britain and to Scandinavia, explored a new trading route around the coast of Africa. They sailed down to the Cape of Good Hope and then north again, and discovered fat pickings in trade with India, Persia, and China.

There was an island in the Orient with a natural harbour that was destined to become a great trading port. North of it was a vast continent ruled over by the Ming Dynasty. But communications were poor, transport was slow, roads were mere tracks and the rulers of China had little contact with their people. The islanders were self-supporting and independent, almost a race apart from those far to the north. They were tough, individualist, and progressive. They prospered on shipping and learned the customs of men from other lands. But the price to be paid for the pickings from commerce was danger and strife. Pirates and slave-traders, as well as roving brigands and private armies, threatened their existence. Bloody brute force often clinched a trading deal, and robbery by force of arms stole the plums of commerce. The Portuguese, long famed as valiant seamen, landed an army upon the island and for long years monopolised its rich trading fruits. In the nineteenth century the island was leased by China for ninety-nine years to Great Britain. It was then named Hong Kong.

The fifteenth century was harsh upon man. Life expectation was low and the death rate high. Few lived to their fifties, and the maimed, the lame, and the blind were abundant. Hygiene and sanitation were unknown, and plagues scythed down the living in great swathes. There was little law and order; pirates and mercenary soldiers ruled with naked steel. Slavery, serfdom, and extreme poverty were commonplace. Life was cheap, and pain and sickness rife.

Upon this island a boy was born to a poor family. When he grew older he looked around him and saw misery with a deeper compassion than other people. Poverty, misery and suffering touched him so deeply that he dedicated himself to alleviating man's sufferings. While others concentrated upon doing their best to outwit others, this boy studied the illnesses of men. There was no science of medicine, and no academically skilled medical practitioners. But there were men who attended the sick for a fee and who might be called doctors. The boy assisted them. He learned their healing methods, and they taught him what they had learned during a lifetime of trial and error. The boy grew older and wiser in the ways of illness. In time he became Dr Fu Lin Chang.

Leah Doctors, allowing herself to be used as an instrument, went into a trance and talked into my tape-recorder. But her voice was the softly accented tone of Dr Fu Lin Chang. He talked about his previous existence on earth five hundred years ago. He described the harshness of life then, the insanitary conditions, and the miserable lack of medical knowledge. There were no schools, few could read and write, and universities were beyond dreams. A doctor then healed the sick to the best of his ability, using instinct and scraps of knowledge he had gained from older doctors, and his skill in acupuncture, surgery, and treatment often restored the health of the sick.

Dr Chang worked in a centre that could perhaps be called a hospital. It was an area covered by a canvas awning stretched over a long row of bamboo rods. Sick people were brought there and left lying upon the ground to get better; or die. It was there that Dr Chang cared for the sick with such instinctive skill and devotion that after some years he became the head doctor of this 'hospital', and its administrator.

Dr Chang recorded:

Naturally, our resources were limited. We used only herbs and acupuncture in those days. If we had to amputate an arm or leg, the best we could do was to mix our patient a strong potion of herbs. This dulled the pain of our patients. Anaesthetics were unknown and it was impossible to avoid causing pain to patients. Often, the shock of pain to a nervous system was so great that it contributed to death. Many died while we were operating. As a surgeon I was called upon to perform all the operations that are practised nowadays. But I had to operate with only the crude knives and instruments available in those days. The work was hard and placed a great strain upon me. But I couldn't neglect it. There were always people who urgently needed a doctor's care and surgery.

All that happened a long time ago. It's a long time to remember back. But I know I had an uncanny flare for understanding the human body, and how it works. This was coupled with my burning zeal to do all I could for my patients. I couldn't select them, nor specialise. They were too many, and their illnesses so varied. I treated patients as they came, one for a disease, one for a wound, and another for a mental disorder, or a broken arm. It was inevitable I learned more about all the types of illnesses humans suffer than many men.

Dr Chang regards his long, hard years on earth as a valuable background for his later work from the spirit world. He lived to what was in those days the unusually ripe age of seventy-two. When he passed over into the spirit world he carried on working in a spirit hospital. Dr Chang described for me the spirit world into which he had entered:

The spirit world is a replica of earth. Here too we have hospitals and other institutions. And it is all very necessary. For example: a person who has suffered a serious accident on earth and has lost a limb, often needs special treatment when he arrives in the spirit world. When that person 'dies', he enters the spirit world with the loss of his limb indelibly branded on his mind. He does not realise that his spirit body is perfect. He therefore needs treatment while he adapts to his new spirit life. He enters one of our hospitals. We have no conception of 'time' in the spirit world that can be related to 'time' on earth. I cannot say how long he would be a patient. For a long period I worked in such hospitals, receiving and treating newcomers to the spirit world. I was happy at this work. All the patients I treated were in great need of help.

But having seen so much suffering on earth, it had always been my hope that I would find a way to ease the suffering of those who had not yet entered the spirit world. This is not so easy as one might think. Spirit doctors can mingle with those on earth and are sometimes able to give them direct healing. But first, they must be able to establish the right kind of contact with them. If a spirit doctor wishes to provide an earthly being with continuous healing – which is often necessary in the treatment of 'incurable' diseases – it is essential for the spirit doctor to work through a suitable medium on earth. And it must be a medium whose vibrations are closely attuned to those of the spirit doctor; so that he can work swiftly and effectively.

Dr Chang explained that it is very difficult for a spirit doctor to find a completely suitable medium. He searched for her a long time before he found Leah. And then she was a child. But he believed she could be trained to become a useful instrument to help him with his work of healing. The most difficult part of the training had been in synchronising their vibrations until they blended satisfactorily. He'd worked with Leah for ten years without Leah having any awareness of him. He'd been obliged to enlist the help of other spirits. Leah's childhood love for animals, and her healing of them, had been part of her early training. The spirit guide, White Feather, had helped to prepare her for spiritual healing when she became an adult.

Once he'd been able to form an affinity with Leah, Dr Chang had had no difficulty in transmitting his healing powers through her. She possessed great compassion for those who suffered; she had a selfless urge to give of herself completely to help others. The love she felt for animals was reciprocated. They sensed her love and returned it. When they were sick, they felt drawn to her, knowing instinctively that she would give them comfort.

While Dr Chang groomed Leah to be his healing medium, he worked hard in the spirit world to prepare himself for the healing work on earth that they would undertake in unison. He studied the most up-to-date methods being used in spirit hospitals to heal people on earth.

In the spirit world I brought myself up-to-date with the latest healing techniques. The spirit world, too, undergoes changes, even though you may not think so. It is progressive change. While I was preparing in the spirit world for my work on earth, we were trying out new ways to reach you. My colleagues in the spirit world are still continuing to do so.'

Dr Chang then described how the modern methods used by those in the spirit world have been overhauled to help cure mortals on earth:

We now use spirit healing power which we convert into healing rays. By converting spirit healing power into healing rays we can focus them in ways that cure the human body. If a man or woman is a psychic, he or she can see the healing rays. Leah can see them; she can also see their various colours. When we are treating a diabetic we use five healing rays. When one is absorbed, we use the next, and so on until all five rays are exhausted. By then the excess blood-sugar has been drawn out and the pancreas strengthened.

In healing the eyes, Dr Chang explained, an entirely different treatment pattern is used. The spirit doctors have worked out treatment patterns for most diseases and illnesses.

In the spirit world, everything is *thought*. Nothing exists apart from *thought*. Our healing rays are operated by *thought* transference. I realise this is most difficult for you to understand – probably impossible for you to understand. But it is the only correct explanation of how our healing rays function. And *you* have evidence that healing rays do cure some people in *your* world. You've learned how victims of medically incurable diseases can be cured by us.

Dr Chang then explained that he is the only spirit doctor who controls Leah; he always has a staff of at least five other spirit colleagues working with him. A spirit operation is performed much in the same way that an earthly surgeon operates in a hospital theatre, assisted by qualified staff. Dr Chang described some of his spirit assistants: Mary is a Sister of Mercy who lived in England; Foo Lun Won is a Chinese medical assistant; another is a Red Indian named White Feather who helped train Leah for her vocation; a fourth helper is Simon, a Jew from Palestine; the fifth is Mustapha from Egypt; and the sixth a Negro named Zamboa. These spirits not only help Dr Chang to operate the healing rays; they also help to boost the strength of the spirit power which the healing rays emit. The psychic power possessed by Leah is also drawn upon to help give the necessary power to the healing rays.

Dr Chang said there are many things about the spirit world which are quite impossible to explain, because an explanation would be beyond my understanding. How can you explain a spotlight to a primitive savage? Dr Chang tried very hard to help me understand the difficulties he faced when communicating through a medium. He used metaphors that helped me dimly to understand.

When I first came back from the spirit world to this earth, I *couldn't* stay here long. The atmosphere was too heavy for me to bear. It was extremely depressing. I worked with Leah, trying to harmonise our vibrations. But I couldn't endure it for long. Suddenly, I had to go. Naturally, Leah was taken by surprise. She wondered what had happened to me. But later I was able to devise a somewhat coarser body – I speak symbolically – which was able to withstand the pressures of the atmosphere better. With it, I was able steadily to increase the length of time I could spend on earth. Little by little I acclimatised myself to the earth's atmosphere and now, with resolution, I can stay as long as I am needed. I can even heal some people now without using Leah as a medium. I do so whenever it is possible. I refrain from keeping Leah in trance for long periods of time because when she is actively in contact with me it drains her psychic power. I prefer to use her power solely for healing, instead of dispersing it without its serving a useful purpose.

7

How Dr Chang
Heals the Sick

MODERN MAN IS mentally geared up to the idea that rays can be used in medicine. The rays of the sun reach everywhere on earth and spread health and life. Without the sun's rays, all living things on earth would eventually die. For many years, X-rays have been in common use by doctors, who highlight the human skeleton, study bone-fractures, and examine diseased organs. Ultra-violet rays and gamma-rays are in constant use in hospitals, doctors' surgeries and private homes. The rays emitted by radium are used in the treatment of cancer. Healing rays used in the way Dr Chang describes them cannot be a novel idea to modern man. If men are ready to accept that a spirit world exists, then spiritual power healing rays would be precisely the kind of healing method we would expect a spirit doctor to use.

'The healing rays are multi-coloured,' explained Dr Chang. 'We must decide which colour to use, and the degree of strength of the ray, in respect of each individual patient. We must also take account of the stage of the illness the patient suffers. Using our healing rays upon humans on earth, is an exact science. It requires long and serious study. Leah has little technical knowledge of these rays. She could neither focus nor control them. We have to do all that from over here. But we *couldn't* do it *without* Leah, and we also draw on her psychic power.'

I asked Dr Chang about the cure of Anne Winne.* Although that had taken place seventeen years earlier, Dr Chang remembered all the

* See page 37

details: 'That lady's healing was so effective because we were quickly able to focus our healing rays directly upon her spirit. I'd asked Leah to bring me a hunchback to cure because we know that if we can direct our healing rays on to a patient's spirit, the hump will dissolve away and the spine will straighten.'

Dr Chang also performs 'spirit operations'. 'We have to bring our own knives with us from the spirit world.' Dr Chang explained. 'Spirit operations are quite a different technique from healing with healing rays. We operate on the spirit body with spirit instruments much in the same way as your surgeons work in hospital theatres. The difference is that *our method is completely painless* for the patient. We cut away any spirit growths, but because the patient does not physically suffer the shock of flesh surgery, they make a swift, if not instantaneous, recovery, depending on how fast the operation transfers from the spirit body on to the patient's physical body.'

Dr Chang said with considerable emphasis: 'We are always careful about claiming we can cure *all* our patients. Your doctors on earth are cautious about this, too. They do the best they can, as we do here; and we are more than content if we meet with success. Your doctors know their limitations and so do we, although our limitations are not neccessarily the same as those of your earth doctors.'

I asked Dr Chang what illness he can – or alternatively, cannot – cure. 'Almost all illnesses can be cured by our healing rays,' he replied. 'And we can almost always effect a healing. But a great deal depends upon the patient. If the patient consciously, or subconsciously, generates a resistance to our healing, the rays cannot penetrate deep enough into his spirit and do their work.

'I'll try to describe how the Healing Rays take effect.

'Let us suppose that a patient's shoulders and upper arms are stiff with arthritis. We will know this and graduate the healing rays to disperse the acids and impurities. If he has a chest complaint, like asthma or bronchitis, we use orange, yellow, and red rays. The green rays are used on the nerve centres. But *it is essential to know precisely where to focus the rays; and the degree of power they must emit.* We must then ask the patient to return for another healing session. We then take account of the healing progress we have already made, and try again. We are learning all the time we are healing. We are constantly learning from experience, and growing more skilful.'

Dr Chang claimed that he has healed kidneys, livers, and stomachs as well as curing cancer and leukaemia. He has mended broken bones, made them knit swiftly, and performed spirit operations for appendicitis, stomach ulcers, and hernia.

Dr Chang said he usually performs spirit operations on patients who have a growth and who are dreading a surgical operation. On occasions a number of spirit operations are necessary before the growth is completely removed. And spirit operations have to reach the patients' spirit before satisfactory results can be obtained.

Dr Chang assumed he had difficulty in getting over this explanation to me, so he elaborated: 'We work on the physical body of the patient until he *feels* it. That feeling goes through to his spirit. The spirit is the personality of a person. All your *feelings* are your spirit. Both our healing rays and spirit operations must penetrate through the subconscious into the spirit. If they cannot reach the spirit, there is only partial success, or failure. The healing rays have to be powerful if they are to penetrate deep enough into the spirit. If the power is insufficient, the patient cannot be cured. That is why it is impossible to cure some patients. They cannot absorb the healing rays, or spirit operations, because some strong resistance in them prevents our healing from reaching their spirit deeply enough. I like my medium to touch my patients by laying on her hands, because her touch conveys a healing sensation. Her touch conveys to the patient that she is emitting a healing power. This helps the healing rays to penetrate through to the spirit.'

In answer to my next question, Dr Chang explained: The source of *all* spiritual healing power, and of good, is – God. The word God means different things to different people. Children think of God as a benevolent old gentleman with a long white beard and smiling down with kindly eyes from somewhere up there. But this image is unacceptable to most adult minds, and people substitute for it a variety of different conceptions. I wanted to know what conception Dr Chang adopted:

'Dr Chang', I said, 'This is a blunt question. You say the source of your healing power is God. That's a word with many different interpretations. What do *you* mean by God?'

'What is God? Shall we say Mother Nature?' Dr Chang said. 'God is the Ultimate Power. God is Spiritual Power. God is Divine Power. God is the Bright Light of all Sources of Understanding.'

8

The Source of Healing Power

I T HAD BECOME evident that it was a waste of time for Dr
Chang to try to tell me what *he* meant by God. Dr Chang
could only communicate with me in words; and the words to convey
his meaning do not exist. Even if they had existed, they would have
been beyond my understanding. Sound cannot be described to a person
who was born deaf.

It was inevitable, I suppose, that my searching investigation of Leah's
healing power would smash against the rock of faith. There are many
happy people who simply *believe.* They do so sincerely and with
unshakeable conviction. They do not need reason. I am *not* one of these
happy people. I must ferret out the basic facts about 'faith healing' and
'spiritual healing rays' and weigh them carefully. A fellow-journalist
once said of me that I wouldn't agree I had five fingers on my hand
unless a chartered accountant certified it.

What were the *facts* I'd learned about Dr Chang's healing rays and
spirit operations?

First, and most striking, was that miraculous healing *seemed* to occur
in Leah's orbit. Whether these healings actually took place can be
debated, of course. But I'd examined an impressive array of cases that
indicated that many patients had been told by hospitals and doctors that
they were incurable, whereas they confirmed they recovered health after
healing sessions with Leah Doctors and Dr Chang. There was also my
own personal experience. After one healing session with Leah and Dr

Chang, my eyesight improved. While investigating Dr Chang, I was continuing treatment and my vision was improving steadily.*

Secondly, Leah Doctors was a medium. She stated that she was controlled by a spirit while in a trance. That she entered into a state of semi-trance, I did not doubt. This is not an unusual occurrnce in our world. Many hypnotists and doctors can guide a subject into a state of trance. We don't know *how* it happens; but we do know that it *does* happen. The trance-like state has been induced and witnessed so often that it is scientifically accepted as a fact. But then comes 'possession'. What about that?

When hypnosis occurs, the hypnotist seems to 'control' the entranced person. Suggestions made by the hypnotist to the entranced person are accepted by him. If a doctor suggests to a hypnotised patient that there is a pleasant warm glow in the left foot, the patient will feel the glow. If the doctor then suggests that this warm glow is steadily becoming a warm numbness, that increasingly there is no sensation in the foot whatsoever except the warm numbness, the hypnotised patient will accept this too. The subject's foot becomes pleasantly numb to all sensations, and a painless operation can be performed upon the foot without the use of anaesthetic.

Do these doctors and hypnotists exercise an influence over their entranced subjects that might be called 'control'? In a limited sense they do. It is evident that a hypnotised subject is capable of feats which he would find impossible unless entranced.

But a hypnotist is a hypnotist! He is a person of livin flesh and blood. Leah insists she is 'controlled' by a spirit; and, while we may concede she is controlled, who or what controls her, needs thinking about.

Leah says she is controlled by the spirit of a man who once lived. No *living* person seems to have any precise scientific knowledge of what happens to human beings when they die. We are convinced, however, that after death the physical human body begins to decompose and decay. If anything remains, it may be 'thoughts' or a 'soul' or a 'spirit'.

---

* On the other hand, my wife, Pearl, had several healing sessions with Leah Doctors, and each time Dr Chang focused his healing rays upon her and also performed a number of spirit operations. Although she had the determination to be cured by spiritual healing and thus was in the 'right frame of mind to enable the healing rays and spirit operations to reach her spirit thoroughly', and although she was repeatedly assured that her complaint would be cured, she did *not* show *any* signs of improvement. Apart from just having wasted time and money, she was utterly disappointed.

A human being without 'thoughts' is incomplete; everyone who lives seethes with 'thoughts'. They are the motivating power of the body, we believe. But despite man's many achievements, we have not yet learned what a thought really is. We believe thoughts exist although we cannot prove it. No scientist has been able to hold a thought between his tweezers, pin it down upon an operating-table, and dissect it. So when people die, there is no scientific test that can show what happens to their thoughts. Do they disintegrate too? Or do thoughts continue to have some form of existence?

Atheists assert that nothing survives death. Leah Doctors, and others, assert that the spirit lives. You can toss a coin to decide who's right. Neither side can prove their claim; nor prove the other party to be mistaken. The atheists who insist that death means complete extinction cannot provide a scrap of material evidence to support their theory – it is impossible to prove a negative, anyway. But after weighing all available theories, perhaps the scales do tilt in favour of Leah Doctors and other mediums. Leah's claim that she is controlled by a spirit is simply a personal statement, which has little factual value. Many people could, and have made, similar statements. In the Middle-Ages so many people were 'possessed' that an alarmed Roman Catholic Church launched the Holy Inquisition. Those who were 'possessed' were accused of witchcraft. The penalty for witchcraft was being burned alive at the stake, and common sense suggests that few people would want to suffer this painful death. Nevertheless, hundreds of people did seem unable to prevent themselves from being 'possessed'. Some martyrs were willing to die at the stake to prove *this* or *that*. But it is reasonable to assume that at least some were possessed unwillingly.

Leah's claim that she is controlled by a spirit is either true or untrue. Attempting to prove that she is *not* controlled, is trying to prove a negative. But can Leah *prove* she is controlled?

Leah does produce some indirect kind of proof. She says that the spirit who controls her can heal the sick. To strengthen her case, she adds that not only can the sick be healed, but also *people who are suffering from medically incurable diseases!* In other words, she says she can heal by means not known to *living* men!

If Leah heals the incurably sick – and she produces many cases which support her claim that she has done so through her mediumship – it is evidence beyond man's understanding. Leah does not *prove* she is controlled by a spirit. But if Leah says her inexplicable healing gift is provided by the spirit who controls her, she has some tangible evidence of healing to back up her claim.

As an objective investigator, I have focussed my attention upon the evidence presented to me. Leah says she is contolled by the spirit of a Chinese doctor who died five hundred years ago. There is *(disputable)* evidence that, through Leah, Dr Chang has healed the incurably sick. By making herself available to me as an instrument of communication, Leah enabled me to communicate with the spirit that controls her. I was even allowed to tape-record the interviews.

I have no sound reason to believe I communicated with the spirit of a Chinese doctor who died five hundred years ago. But neither can I find a sound reason to prove that I did *not!* On the fragmentary evidence I possess, I would be unjustified in denying the spirit existence of Dr Chang. But likewise, I do not feel I have a sound enough reason to assert that Leah is controlled by a spirit.

If a space-probe flashes back to earth a message that it has encountered a new type of life form on Jupiter, I cannot deny that it is possible. I would have no sound reason for believing the statement. But equally, I would have no factual evidence to prove it impossible. The scientists, specialists, and computers that interpret the space probe's radio signals into commonsense language, would perform for the space-probe the services that Leah claims she performs for Dr Chang.

But I have an advantage over the space-probe scientists. They must depend solely upon scientific data, whereas I can ask all kinds of unscientific questions and receive answers.

Dr Chang confirmed to me that he is a spirit. He said that everything in the spirit world is thought. This makes some sense in a strange way. Everybody has enjoyed daydreams. For all of us our minds have conjured up pictures of the kind of world in which we would like to live, and the pleasurable incidents we would like to have happen. Probably every boy and girl in love have pictured themselves happily embraced. The drabness of our life can be transformed for a time by our thoughts. Every optimist who fills in his football coupon visualises himself as wealthy. A plain girl can convince herself *in her mind* that she is greatly admired. The quiet, unassertive man can picture himself as a dominant personality, moulding his own destiny and that of others. Our thoughts can create our own ideal world that we will be happy to live in. With our thoughts we can even build a mental picture of a brick wall and see its dimensions and its colour, and sense its strength.

What we can't do is rap on it with out knuckles and feel its solidity.

So, when Dr Chang says his spirit world is a world of thought, this is not beyond our understanding. Nor is it impossible. For all we know, we may all actually live in a thought world. Can we *prove* that when we rap a brick wall with our knuckles we actually *feel* it? Isn't is possible that feeling too is made of thoughts?

If we go along with Dr Chang's statement a little way, purely as a mental exercise, we can hold our judgment in abeyance until we reach his grand total. The grand total of a list of numbers can be checked mathematically. A cross-check can prove that it is a correct total. But the total Dr Chang provides for us, *cannot* be checked.

Dr Chang's grand total is – God.

When Dr Chang uses the word 'God' he is using a symbol that Western man has long used to explain the supernatural.

Throughout his earthly existence, man has used 'God' to describe events beyond his understanding. When storms raged and the black heavens thundered, the Norseman provided an explanation of this phenomenon. It was the great god Thor, striding through the heavens and hammering the clouds with his giant club. When crops were bad, primitive Aztecs offered up human sacrifices to appease their god and restore fertility to the land. When people inexplicably died off like flies, it was not attributed to the spread of contagious diseases, but to the wrath of God for man's evilness. When Jesus Christ healed the sick, it was because he was the Son Of God. When healthy people died suddenly, suffering acute stomach pains, it was God's Will, and not attributed to appendicitis until surgery became a science.

Dr Chang uses the word 'God' as man has always used the word – to explain the inexplicable. But Dr Chang qualifies it. He adds that the source of his healing power is Mother Nature; the Ultimate Power; the Spiritual Power; the Divine Power. He also says: 'God is the Bright Light of Understanding'.

Dr Chang is virtually saying that Ultimate Power is Total Knowledge. And he is calling this 'God'. Most scientists would probably feel themselves in agreement with this definition of God. A Total Knowledge of the Laws of Nature would reveal the Ultimate Power!

Modern man has learned a great deal about the Laws of Nature. They rule man's existence. The Law of Gravity, discovered by Newton, which explains why apples fall from trees, rules all our lives. Yet man is rarely conscious that the Law of Gravity is operating unless he is butterfingered. Modern practical tests, proving that man is weightless in outer space, do not disprove gravity. On the contrary. They have *proved* the Law of Gravity.

Man's existence depends upon the ceaseless operating of the law of cause and effect; the transfer of energy from one object to another. This law enables man to breathe, or to flick a fly off his cheek by reflex action. Every action of human beings is governed by this natural law. It influences a speck of dust, activates an atom bomb and binds our solar system to the universe.

If natural laws are so powerful, and yet so difficult to discern, can it be wise to deny that a Law of Nature can exist which may control the thought existence of *Man Before Death,* and *Man after Death?*

What happens to man's 'thoughts' when he dies? Is it possible that after death man's thoughts have continued existence in a thought world or spirit world, the kind of daydream world in which all men have lived for a time?

Healing the incurable is inexplicable – on earth. But Dr Chang's explanation of how it is done is not inexplicable. He asserts that he uses healing rays. This is a method man has used for many years to heal the sick. What Dr Chang doesn't, or cannot, explain is the source of power for his healing rays. He says it is the Ultimate Power, Spiritual Power, Divine Power – the Bright Light of all Sources of Understanding.

It is the source of power that it is difficult to understand. But then, a primitive savage would find it difficult to understand an engineer's explanation of how a combustion engine works.

I have tried to investigate Dr Chang's and Leah Doctors' healing powers objectively. I have tried to discover how and why Dr Chang uses healing rays and performs spirit operation and Leah possesses healing gifts.

I have been unable to find any convincing explanation. Leah's Spirit Guide theory cannot be proved. Equally, there is nothing to disprove it. Once again you can toss your coin – heads you believe Leah and Dr Chang, tails you don't!

But the coin is very slightly weighed in favour of Dr Chang and Leah.

And both Dr Chang and Leah Doctors insist that the healing of incurable diseases still goes on through Leah's mediumship!

If medically incurable sufferers *can* be healed by Dr Chang through

Leah Doctors it is a great boon to mankind. People would be *mad* if they didn't take every advantage of this phenomenon. No man has died of hunger because he didn't understand how apples grow on trees. No medically incurable persons need suffer pain and die because they don't understand the spiritual healing methods being used. But people who can be healed by orthodox medicine should *always* consult their doctor first before deciding to rely entirely on spiritual healing miracle cures.

Spritual healing can be magic, miracles, self-delusion, Spiritualism, or any other name invented on the spur of the moment.

But if spiritual healing *works*, and there is evidence that often it does, we should take every advantage of it.

Why spiritual healing works, and how, can be learned at leisure in the following parts of this book.

9

'So Many People Could be Healed'

'FINDING THE RIGHT medium on earth through whom I can work efficiently was extremely difficult,' said Dr Chang. 'I was searching for a needle in a haystack. A hundred or a thousand people might at first seem very suitable. Then, after a time, I'd learn there were disharmonies in our vibrations which it was impossible for me to overcome. I spent many years searching before I discovered Leah. All spirit doctors who want to help people on earth face the same problem. It's extremely difficult to find an ideal medium. The search for them is constant. This is the reason there are not many more spirit doctors and surgeons helping people on earth.

'I found Leah when she was a child and began training her without her knowledge. Other spirit colleagues helped me to prepare her, including White Feather, who was sometimes directly in contact with her. And finally, seventeen years ago, she was ready to work with me. We are an excellent partnership, and very happy together. She's very healthy and will live a long time; so we can look forward to relieving a great deal of human suffering.'

I talked with Dr Chang about 'absent healing'. This is another aspect of spiritual healing. The method is simple. The sick person writes or telephones to the spiritual healer, gives his name and address, and asks for absent healing. Distance is no obstacle. Application for absent healing can be made from New York, Sydney, or Timbuctu. Absent healing is difficult for an investigator to check upon. To read a letter from X in Australia asking for absent healing, and then read another letter of a later date saying the writer is grateful and completely cured, is little *proof* of anything, except that letters have been written.

But large numbers of people *do* write afterwards and say that they are completely cured, and fit and well years after they received absent healing.

Very often, an illness is aggrevated by the patient's mental attitude. Practising doctors are well aware of this. In many cases a doctor's 'bedside manner' contributes much more to the recovery of the patient than the contents of the prescribed bottle of medicine. Applying for absent healing and then being informed by letter that they are receiving it, could be a great mental comfort to many sick people, and make a great contribution to their recovery.

And Dr Chang insisted that *serious* illnesses can be cured by absent healing – *sometimes;* he explained:

> When Leah receives a patient's address it enables us to locate him swiftly. We attend him during his sleep-state. Because he has applied for our help he has the right mental attitude that enables us to give him treatment in his sleep-state. Often it is not as effective as Leah laying on hands, and adding her power to ours. But we have done a lot of absent healing and we do have considerable success with it in many parts of the world.

> One sad case was a little girl who was fatally ill. She had leukaemia. This child's mother was so distraught that she telephoned Leah from her home in Ireland. The little girl was in hospital, unconscious and dying. The mother telephoned at six o'clock in the evening. The doctors had warned her that the little girl might die at any time. We naturally did everything in our power to heal her. At ten o'clock that evening she suddenly regained consciousness. From that moment onwards she steadily improved. That was four years ago. Today she goes to school and is as healthy as any other child.

> In absent healing the patient cannot know we are at his side giving him healing treatment. Without Leah as a medium we can judge if absent healing is effective only by the patient's reports about his improvement in health.

Dr Chang switched from absent healing to spiritual healing on the whole:

> It is a weighty claim to make, but we *can* cure cancer. But we cannot do so completely efficiently if there has already been intervention by a surgeon, or if radium rays have been used. It *is*

possible for us to cure cancer in one treatment. Where there is a cancerous growth we do not heal the growth; instead, we extract it from the body through the bowels, or through the mouth. Afterwards we use healing rays to heal any injury to tissues caused by the growth, or by its removal.

Cancer is a dreaded illness, and public feeling is so strongly opposed to raising false hopes in cancer sufferers that cancer cures are not publicised. As a result, many cancer victims are unaware of the help that spiritual healing can give them. It's a great pity. So many unfortunate people could be cured of cancer, or have their suffering alleviated, if they knew where to come. This book you're writing will, I hope, help some of these people.

Dr Chang agreed that although there are many spiritual healers, only very few are proficient at healing. He said:

Spiritual healing ability depends a great deal upon harmony-vibrations between the spirit doctor and his medium. As I've already said, an efficient partnership between medium and spirit doctor is difficult to achieve. If the *rapport* between them is not ideal, their healing suffers and is sometimes indifferent. Because it is so difficult to find an ideal combination of medium and spirit doctor, good spiritual healers are rare.

Dr Chang believes he and Leah are a rare combination, and that together they can cure leukaemia, many other forms of cancer, and tumours of the brain. 'I *can* cure these. I *can* do it,' said Dr Chang. 'It may sound boastful; but I *can* do it!'

Among other illnesses he was confident he could cure, Dr Chang cited broken bones:

In some cases I have knitted bones together within a few hours. It isn't always possible to heal quickly. But if a patient has a broken arm or leg bone, and the vibrations are right, it's possible to knit the broken ends overnight. We have done this a number of times.

Loss of hair and approaching baldness are human ailments Dr Chang believes it is important to heal.

When man's hair grows thin, it is a natural process. We could probably stimulate new growth if we tried, but we prefer to concentrate upon serious illnesses. We've never treated baldness in men. But it's a very different matter whan a lady's hair begins to fall out. Much more is involved than the loss of hair. A lady facing baldness can become seriously disturbed mentally and suffer acutely from shock, worry, and nerves. Grave illnesses often result from small causes. Frequently, in such cases, the only healing treatment is to restore the growth of hair. It's a long healing process. It requires weekly healing sessions. It takes a month, or five weeks, before regrowth of hair begins. But we do restore healthy growth of hair in the cases we treat.

Dr Chang described one of the spirit instruments he uses in spirit surgery:

It's a long rod. About the size of a long pencil. It has no substance, of course. In a case of deafness, for example, we insert it in one ear, right through the head, and out of the other ear. Leah then places her hands upon the patient's ears, holding the spirit rod there with her own psychic power. Then the rod glows and vibrates. It shimmers a bright red. The patient will afterwards describe a burning sensation in his head and ears. When Leah removes her hands and the rod is withdrawn, the patient feels as though something in the head has been opened up, and then closed again.

We use the spirit rod for many illnesses. It's very useful for operating upon a child's tonsils. It can restore full health to the tonsils, and eliminate the need of cutting them out.

To describe any spirit instrument to you means little. You can't even begin to understand its working principles. Leah has co-operated with us for seventeen years and understands almost nothing about the healing work we perform through her. You must realise that we in the spirit world have a vast reserve of knowledge we can draw upon. *How* it works is not really important. What *is* important is that our healing *does work*. And anyone can investigate and prove this for himself. To heal is our objective and we use all the means we have. And all the time we are learning better ways to bridge the gap between your world and ours. We *must,* if we are to reduce and eliminate your human sufferings.

* * *

There are mediums who, with the help of the spirit people, make drawings and paintings of those in the spirit world. The psychic artist,

McDonald, painted a spirit picture of Dr William Lang. This painting has been compared with a photograph taken of Dr Lang before he died; it is confirmed that Mr McDonald never saw this photograph. The similarity between the painting and the photograph was astonishing. A number of psychic artists have asked Dr Chang if they can enter into spiritual harmony with him, and draw him. Dr Chang has always politely but firmly declined. I asked Dr Chang *why* he refused to be painted?

It is quite true. Many psychic artists have asked Leah's permission to draw, or paint, my likeness. But I opposed the suggestion. Leah respects my wishes and declined the offers. There are good reasons. Above all, you must realise I am merely a humble instrument of God and his spiritual healing power. Neither Leah nor myself are important, except as humble healing instruments. Only God is important. Neither Leah nor myself wish to divert attention to ourselves, and away from the Ultimate Power. People must realise that we are merely the means, and not the cause, of healing. There is an unhappy tendency in *your* world for humans to worship symbols, instead of the true Ultimate Power. It is sad to think of those men whose photographs have been widely publicised for mass worship. Humans have an unhappy knack of revering photographs. It isn't so bad, I suppose, when every home bears a photograph of the royal family. But think of all the attention that was diverted away from the true Ultimate Power, and instead directed upon photographs of Stalin, Hitler, and Mussolini.

There is a secondary reason why I don't wish my likeness to be drawn or painted. It is again related to the human way of thinking. A doctor who is tall and imposing, and perhaps a little severe and abrupt, gives his patients great confidence. They feel he is clever and capable. The patient's confidence in his doctor plays an important part in his healing. Now, there is little about me that would inspire confidence in my patients. A physical likeness of me might dispel some patients' confidence. This would build up a resistance to healing and would make our work more difficult.

When I pressed him, Dr Chang gave me, half-humourously, a verbal description of himself:

If you were to see me, as some of my patients who are psychic have seen me, you, too, would be unimpressed. I am only five feet two inches tall. I have to look up at my patients to talk to them. I am very thin, almost fragile, and I have a long, bony, thin-skinned face. My eyes are brown and placed very far apart. My short, white beard dribbles to a point. I wear a round, tight skull cap and a long, enveloping purple robe. I do not look impressive. If a surgeon were to prepare an operation by setting out blunted, rusty scalpels, he would alarm his patients. I would look blunted and rusty to many people. But appearance shouldn't matter, because I and Leah are but humble instruments of God, of the true Ultimate Power. Nevertheless, it is very important that we inspire confidence in our patients. Does this answer your question?

My interviews with Dr Chang are recorded on tape. Dr Chang spoke through Leah. She talks in an accented voice that is quite different from her own. If all this is a fake it is a very laboriously and painfully fabricated hoax. A hoax that serves no useful purpose, either to the hoaxer, or to those taken in. The only important claim made by Dr Chang is that he can heal the sick. But to set up this spirit medium interview simply to make this statement would be quite pointless. It gives no backing whatsoever to Leah's claim that she heals the sick.

Moreover, Dr Chang's and Leah's healing can, in some ways, be put to a practical test. Therefore, it is not very important to ask myself if Leah is disguising her voice so that she can hoax me. The much more important question to ask, and have answered, is: Do Dr Chang and Leah Doctors heal the sick?

10

'Stop Healing – or Quit!'

TO LEAH AND Jack Doctors the public healing demonstrations in the Alliance Hall were financially costly. But
they led directly to the healing of confirmed diabetics. The first was Mr
L G Gingell. Leah told me: He had been a diabetic for twenty-one years.
He was prescribed a weekly intake of seventy-eight units of insulin. He
had a long journey to work, and was so tired at the end of the day that
he was fit only for bed when he arrived home. He was informed by
hospital specialists that there was *no cure* for his illness. It could only be
prevented from getting worse by regular injections of insulin.

Mr Gingell's chronic tiredness, which all diabetics must learn to live
with, increasingly depressed him. He lost the zest for life. He became
a listless machine. He went to work because it was necessary to earn
money to buy food and shelter. The joy of living eluded him. When
he heard about Leah Doctors and her cures of diabetics, he grasped at
this straw of hope desperately. Mr Gingell made his way to Bethune
Road, met Leah Doctors, and stretched out wearily on the couch.

Leah laid hands upon Mr Gingell. She explained how she drew from
Dr Chang a healing power that cured diabetes. Dr Chang then controlled Leah and talked directly to Mr Gingell while Leah moved her
hands over the patient's shoulders, wrists, and thighs. Dr Chang said Mr
Gingell would need a number of treatments to be completely cured.
The patient should make a urine test every morning and when the
result of the test was blue for three mornings in succession, his intake
of insulin could be reduced. Dr Chang warned that insulin reduction
should be adopted only with a medical consultant's approval. The

patient then lay upon his stomach and Dr Chang concentrated healing rays upon the pancreas gland to improve the circulation of blood within it. The treatment lasted half an hour.

On the following day Mr Gingell noticed that he did not tire so quickly. On the fifth morning his urine test showed blue for the third morning in succession. Mr Gingell was booked to see his medical consultant the day before his next healing session with Dr Chang. The medical consultant was sceptical when Mr Gingell reported his urine test. But after making a routine test himself he reduced the prescribed dose of insulin.

The pattern of healing continued until, at the end of eight weeks, Mr Gingell's insulin intake was reduced from the original seventy-eight units to twenty-eight units a week. The treatment continued another four weeks at the end of which Mr Gingell was taken off insulin altogether. He was cured!

Mr Gingell was no longer obliged to adhere to a rigid diet and he arrived home from work full of energy and eager to live.

* * *

Helen Grant was thirty-six years of age. She was a diabetic in the care of a hospital. Her illness had reached an advanced stage She had been on a weekly dose of seventy-five units of insulin for several months. But her illness could not be controlled and the weekly dosage was increased to eighty-two units. Even so, the doctors expected her condition to deteriorate. Helen Grant was depressed, suffering extreme nervous tension and contemplated suicide.

A friend of Helen's, knowing she was desperately ill, urged her to visit Leah. The friend had witnessed Leah's public demonstration of healing and had been deeply impressed. Helen Grant became one of Leah's patients. She lay upon the couch and Leah laid her hands on her. Leah frequently had to clean her hands which had drawn off a kind of stickiness. Dr Chang explained to Helen Grant that he was removing a considerable quantity of sugar from her body. He said he could cure her, but it was essential that she visited him regularly. Perhaps ten or twelve times. She'd responded extremely well to his healing rays and she'd soon notice an improvement in her condition.

Helen Grant recalled that Dr Chang displayed a foreknowledge of the future. He told her she had a hospital appointment the following

Friday. Helen confirmed this, wondering how Dr Chang knew about it. Dr Chang then said the medical consultant would be pleased with the improvement in her condition, and would reduce her weekly dosage of insulin by seven units.

At the Friday hospital appointment, as Dr Chang had predicted, Helen Grant's insulin dosage *was* reduced by seven units. The doctor discouraged optimism by adding that the reduction was purely a medical test. He warned that the dosage might have to be increased again.

It wasn't. Helen Grant visited Leah every week, keeping the medium fully occupied drawing out sugar from her body during the treatment. And every week the hospital doctor reduced Helen's intake of insulin. Each healing session lasted half an hour and at the conclusion of the eleventh, Dr Chang told Helen she was completely cured. She already knew this. For weeks she had been rejoicing about her steady improvement of health. She'd forgotten all morbid, suicidal thoughts and was bright and cheerful. She tried to thank Dr Chang but he deflected her gratefulness. 'You mustn't thank *me*,' he said. 'You must thank *God*!'

The hospital doctors confirmed that Helen Grant had lost all her diabetic symptoms, contrary to all their experience of the disease. Although they were pleased for the patient, they were concerned for her future. She was discharged from the hospital, but warned that she must regularly test her urine. At the first hint of a return of her illness, she must report at once to the hospital.

In all the years that have elapsed since Helen Grant's diabetes was cured by Dr Chang, she has not had a return of it. She married a year after her healing and is now in the best of health, living a very full life with her husband and children.

* * *

Leah Doctors' healing sanctuary in Bethune Road became a busy healing centre. As patients told others of their cures, the ringing of the doorbell was frequent. Many hours every day of Leah's time were spent in healing. She was content. She was relieving suffering. The more patients the better.

But the healing sanctuary was in truth only a small room in a first floor flat. Dozens of people rang the doorbell and scaled the stairs. The premises became an ever-open shop and aroused the resentment of the neighbours; especially the new ground-floor tenants who distrusted the 'spooky goings on upstairs'. They registered a firm protest with the houseowner.

The legal position was quite clear. The premises were rented to the Doctors for *residential* purposes *only*. It was unimportant whether or not Leah Doctors asked a fee. Using the flat as a healing sanctuary was considered by the houseowner as running a business and consequently a violation of the contract. The landlord served notice on the Doctors that the flat must be vacated by a certain date. If they failed to comply with the order, they would be evicted.

At that time it was difficult to find a vacant flat or house to let. And it was most unlikely a landlord would permit living accommodation to be used for a healing sanctuary as well. But if Leah was to continue her healing work, it had to be from a base that was known to be a healing centre.

The answer to the Doctors' problem was to buy a property and be free from landlords' restrictions. The snag was that although the Doctors could scrape together weekly repayments on a house purchase, they couldn't raise the capital required for a mortgage deposit.

Leah had now healed many people and among them, many wealthy patients. But not all had contributed to Leah's outgoing expenses and she had no reserve funds. Leah soon learned that some sick people, once healed, quickly lost their gratefulness. Wealthy patients who had been profuse with thanks when Dr Chang healed them through Leah, were disappointingly disinterested when Leah sought small loans to raise a mortgage deposit to keep the healing sanctuary going.

After being adroitly turned down a number of times, Leah ruefully realised she was being over-optimistic. So her thoughts turned to winning the football pools. She didn't understand football. But the competitions in *Reveille* were simple to enter. Leah filled in *Reveille* competitions coupons every week and sent them in. She wasn't expecting to win a fortune, but she might be lucky to win the few hundred pounds she needed for a mortgage deposit.

Time passed. Patients called, were healed and made their modest contributions. The letting agencies monotonously reported they could find the Doctors no alternative living accommodation. The day when the premises must be vacated remorselessly approached. The Doctors were trapped. They would soon have to make a serious decision. They would have to give up the healing sanctuary, or be turned out into the street. Jack Doctors suggested Leah should ask Dr Chang's advice and this is Leah Doctors' description of what happened, transcribed from my tape-recorder:

I asked Dr Chang: 'Dr Chang, will you please help me?' Suddenly he was in front of me. I could see him clearly – his white pointed beard and his purple robe. He nodded his head gravely and said: 'Carry on with the competition in *Reveille*. We will help you.'

I did the competition again that week but purposely didn't think about what I wrote on my entry form. And the following week I had a letter saying I'd won half the prize. It was five hundred pounds. When I held the cheque in my hand I could sense Dr Chang looking over my shoulder. He said: 'Now you have the money for your healing sanctuary. Don't use it for anything else.' It was the few hundred pounds I needed for the mortgage deposit. We'd already chosen the house that would be suitable if we could raise the money. It was in Stamford Hill.

The Westbank Healing Sanctuary in Stamford Hill was to become well known in Britain and abroad.

11

The Westbank Healing Sanctuary

HOPEFUL PATIENTS BEGAN to seek spiritual healing help at the newly established Westbank Healing Sanctuary. Some of these were seriously ill people yet many had minor ailments only.

One of the first Westbank patients was Miss Edith Winter and, somewhat proudly, Leah pointed her out to me as her first spectacular success at the just established sanctuary.

Forty years previously Miss Winter had perforated her ear-drum. Ever since she'd suffered severe bouts of pain and was deaf in one ear. As she grew older the bouts of pain became more frequent and more severe. The doctors could do nothing for her, apart from prescribing pain-relieving drugs. Miss Winter heard about the Westbank Healing Sanctuary and visited Leah. The following is her account of what transpired:

I sat on a chair and as soon as Mrs Doctors placed her hands upon my ears I had the feeling that they were growing hotter and hotter. Then, Dr Chang came through Mrs Doctors. He had a deeper voice and a lisping, Chinese accent. He told me he would put me completely right if I came to Mrs Doctors for treatment five or six times. Then I felt as if some long instrument, some sort of stick, was being pushed through my head from ear to ear, painlessly. Right inside my head I had a hot feeling; and it was as though something was being pushed away. It's impossible to describe the feeling, but it was weird. Yet, at the same time I felt something good was being done to me, and suddenly I was quite sure I was being healed. The treatment lasted about half-an-hour and when it was over I was astonished. I'd been in great pain when I first sat down. I'd grown accustomed to pain after all these years. It was immense relief to feel my pain had almost vanished.'

Miss Winter attended regularly for healing treatment, and after six weeks Dr Chang told her she need not visit him again. Her perforated ear-drum had been healed. Since Miss Winter's last visit to Dr Chang she has been quite free of any pain in her ear, and she can hear perfectly.

* * *

Mrs Marjory Wright was a diabetic who attended hospital for two years. She was thirty years of age, had to observe a strict diabetic diet and inject herself with the given dosage of insulin. One of the hospital nurses privately mentioned to Mrs Wright that some diabetics had been helped by consulting a spiritual healer – Leah Doctors.

Mrs Wright took the hint and had weekly treatments by Dr Chang for three months. Each week her condition improved and her urine tests indicated that the hospital doctor could decrease her insulin intake. At the end of the healing sessions Dr Chang told her she no longer needed insulin, and had no need to stick to a diet. 'Eat and drink whatever you like. You are cured and you will not suffer from this illness again. Tomorrow, at your hospital appointment, your doctor will confirm all I've told you.'

Mrs Wright visited the hospital the following day and was discharged as being no longer in need of diabetic treatment. The doctor warned her she must make regular urine tests and attend hospital if her illness returned. The doctors at this hospital had treated other diabetics who had visited Leah, and were familiar with the phenomenon of a diabetic patient requiring less and less insulin until all symptoms of the disease had vanished. They may even have come to accept that spiritual healing, whatever its methods, could cure diabetics where orthodox medicine could not.

* * *

Mr James Bell, aged sixty-eight, was registered at his hospital for four years as a diabetic patient. His insulin dosage was eighty units.

Mr Bell's treatment at Leah's healing sanctuary lasted six months and then Dr Chang announced his patient was cured. Mr Bell was discharged from hospital after tests showed that he was completely free of diabetic symptoms.

12

Leah Heals in Hospitals

L EAH'S HEALING BECAME known not only to hospital out-patients, but to in-patients too. Many who had been bedridden for weeks and months and who believed their condition was hopeless wrote to Leah's healing sanctuary. She told me:

I used to visit many hospitals. St Thomas's Hospital is a London teaching hospital, and it's from there I received most requests. I also visited Soho Women's Hospital, as well as others.

If a hospital patient required healing from me and Dr Chang, all that was necessary was to ask the doctor in charge for permission for me to visit. As far as I know, a patient's request has never been refused. The only restrictions placed upon me were sensible ones. For example, I wasn't to lay hands upon a patient who had recently undergone an operation, for fear of the danger of infection. But even this was not a restriction because I was able to heal through blankets and sheets.

I became well known at the hospitals. Especially at St Thomas's where I aroused great interest. Sisters and nurses from other wards often came to watch me. The nursing staff were very kind and helpful. They were so pleased at my success in healing patients. Many told me they were amazed at the cures.

Although they shouldn't have done so, the nurses chatted about my work with their patients. If the doctors couldn't keep in check a patient's illness, and the patient was suffering pain without hope of a cure, the nurses mentioned to the patient that I might be able to help. If those patients later asked me for treatment, and if Dr Chang used his healing rays upon them, they improved in health and were later discharged from hospital.

Working in hospitals was very hard, but very rewarding. I'd have been happier if I'd been permitted to visit everybody who was gravely ill. Many hospitalised people need Dr Chang's help. But we could heal only those patients who complied with regulations and requested an appointment. I'd have loved to be free to tour the wards and give healing treatment where it was most needed. I could have cone so much more!

* * *

One of Dr Chang's healings through Leah's mediumship which greatly impressed hospital doctors and nursing staff was the following cancer case.

Mrs Sheila Cummings worked in a Whitehall office, and was in her early forties. She attended hospital for stomach pains. Tests showed she had cancer of the stomach. Surgery might help the patient to some extent, but the doctors feared that the continued growth of the cancer was inevitable. Mrs Cummings was incurable and could not live long. She was warned that she was seriously ill and would probably not recover. She accepted her fate bravely. She was grateful to the hospital for all the care and attention she had received and agreed to undergo surgery, although she knew its pain and discomfort could only delay the inevitable for a few short weeks or months.

A week before Sheila was to undergo surgery, she learned about Leah Doctors from one of the hospital staff. She requested permission for Leah to visit her.

When Leah laid her hands upon Sheila, she was watched by a large group of hospital sisters and nurses. Almost at once Leah was taken over by Dr Chang. As Leah's hands moved gently, Sheila Cummings told the watching nurses she could feel something hot moving around inside her. Dr Chang spoke through Leah and told the patient and the nurses that he was directing healing rays upon the cancerous growth. He said there would be no need for a surgical operation. The healing rays would disperse the cancer.

Dr Chang concentrated his healing rays upon the patient for half-an-hour and then told her he had succeeded in dispersing the cancer. He said pieces of it would be discharged through the bowels. He added he was pleased to discover that the patient was ideally attuned to the healing rays so he had been able to disperse the cancer in *one* healing session. When Leah came out of trance, she assured Mrs Cummings that she was completely cured, and would soon enjoy the benefits of Dr Chang's healing treatment.

For the next few days Mrs Cumming's stools contained lumps of matter, as Dr Chang had predicted. Her pain diminished, and then ceased. Pre-operative tests were made and it was found that Mrs Cummings was no longer in need of surgical intervention. She was eventually discharged from hospital free from any symptoms of cancer. Ever since, Mrs Cummings has enjoyed good health.

* * *

Leah's healings in hospitals attracted the attention of medical consultants from her very first hospital visit; she attended a dying West African patient in St Thomas's Hospital.*

This West African was a government official resident abroad. While on a three-months holiday in Britain, he took the opportunity to consult medical specialists about his health. He was told he had a seriously enlarged heart.

At the end of his holiday, while on his way to the docks to return to West Africa, he collapsed, and was rushed to St Thomas's Hospital. His legs swelled up like balloons and, although the doctors were able to treat the swelling, they could do nothing to heal the cause of his trouble: his enlarged heart.

Leah was asked to attend the West African by one of his relatives. The patient's condition was hopeless. He could neither eat nor drink; even if he spoke in a whisper it placed a dangerous strain upon his heart. The patient's wife had already been warned there was no hope for him, and that she should come to London to make arrangements for his body to be transported to West Africa.

When Leah entered the ward, the patient was in an oxygen tent, which he had occupied for two days. The doctors said only this had helped him survive so long. They did not believe he could last another forty-eight hours.

'He was propped up on pillows and was sweating profusely,' said Leah. 'I've never heard such loud heart-beats. I rested my hand upon his

---

* I have seen the records of this gentleman's case but for personal and political reasons he has withheld permission to publish his name and address.

heart and my hand went backwards and forwards. But all the time it was there it was healing. I gave him healing treatment for about half an hour but there was no visible improvement. I thought I'd arrived too late and that he was too far gone. There are sad cases when nothing can be done to save a patient. But Dr Chang told me not to give up. He said it wasn't hopeless. So I kept my hand on the patient's heart. And very gradually the chest-pounding ceased. After another half an hour or so, the heart was beating normally.'

When this happened, Leah said, the patient looked up at her, immensely relieved. 'Thank God you've come,' he whispered. 'I prayed all day you would come and give me healing treatment. God has answered my prayers. I'm so much better now. I can even breathe easily.'

From then onwards, the West African improved rapidly. Within a few days he had completely recovered. The doctors and medical staff were astonished. They kept him under observation for several days, fearing a relapse. But his recovery was so evident that they soon discharged him from hospital, declaring him fit for the journey to West Africa.

* * *

Although this healing is no more remarkable than many of Dr Chang's and Leah's healings, it had taken place in a London teaching hospital – like the healing of Mrs Eileen Cummings. A great many people heard about it. It had all the marks of a newsworthy story, with banner-headlines SNATCHED BACK FROM DEATH. Reporters visited the hospital, and clamoured for details. They obtained medical reports on the patient's condition, and eyewitness descriptions of his recovery under Leah's healing hands. But they met a set-back when they interviewed the patient. The West African forbade them to publish his name and address, or any details of his private life. So, when the news-story was published in the *Tottenham Herald,* the details of the miraculous recovery were fully described, but the identity of the patient who had come so close to death was not revealed.

But the West African's name is known to me, as is his work in West Africa. He has been frequently in the news for many years, and his strenuous activities confirm that his restored health enables him to labour long hours under high pressures.

13

Moving to Sussex

L EAH'S OWN MOTHER became a patient of Dr Chang. She
was seventy-six years old and suffered chronic bronchitis and
palpitations of the heart. Her doctor told Leah confidentially: 'I'm sorry,
Mrs Doctors; she's old. There isn't much I can do for her. I don't think
she can last long.' He suggested that Leah's mother should enter
Hackney Hospital.

But the old lady had no wish to go into hospital. She said she
depended upon her daughter to give her all the treatment she needed.
Her doctor shrugged his shoulders and smiled ruefully.

Leah gave her mother spiritual healing twice a week for three
months. She improved until she was able to get up and go about. She
lived alone again, visited the cinema, did her own shopping and
house-work, and remained active until the last two weeks of her life.
She died when she was eighty, having outlived her doctor's expectations
by four years.

'Spiritual healing cannot give eternal life,' said Dr Chang. 'It heals,
but yields to the inevitability of death.'

When Leah's mother took to her bed and said she wanted to sleep
a long time, Leah knew it was the end. Dr Chang helped to grant her
mother's last wish – to pass away peacefully in her sleep.

* * *

For four years the Westbank Healing Sanctuary treated dozens of
patients every week. The majority of the healings were satisfying to the

patients but disappointing to those interested only in the sensational. For example, after the birth of her second baby, Mrs Cox was constantly in the care of the hospital. She suffered excruciating pain, and the special corset made for her afforded only slight relief. It was agony for her to sit or walk. After one healing rays treatment from Dr Chang, Mrs Cox discarded her special course and today is still free from the agony she once endured.

Over the years, 'minor' healings, similar to that of Mrs Cox, totalled many hundreds. Human suffering cannot be computed. But Dr Chang and Leah Doctors have helped a great many people live happier and richer lives, and this knowledge has repaid them handsomely for all the long hours thay have devoted to spiritual healing.

But the Westbank Healing Sanctuary had minor drawbacks, and a plan grew in Leah's mind to find another house that would be more convenient for healing. One patient suggested Leah should move from London and its contaminated air to the coast. Leah consulted Dr Chang and he approved. So once again she and her husband began a search for alternative accommodation.

They finally decided upon a house in Brighton, which seemed very suitable. It would provide accommodation for a healing sanctuary and the neighbourhood was acceptable. It was close to the railway station and not too far from the sea. The price was one the Doctors could afford and they decided to make the move. Arrangements were made for the sale of Westbank to provide the mortgage deposit on the new property.

But there were vague doubts in Leah's mind about the new house. When they made their next move they wanted it to be a lasting one so they could set up a permanent healing sanctuary on the south coast. Again Leah consulted Dr Chang who told her she wouldn't move into the house in Brighton. He said she'd move into a house on the other side of Brighton – in Hove.

The Doctors were already involved in negotiations and didn't change their plans. But soon after Leah's discussion with Dr Chang, Jack telephoned excitedly. He was in Hove, had lost his way, and by chance had seen a 'For Sale' board outside a house that looked exactly right for them.

Together they visited 47 Goldstone Villas in Hove. They were both instantly sure it was without doubt the house they needed. They didn't hesitate. They visited their solicitor, gave notice that they wouldn't complete the purchase of the house in Brighton, and contracted to buy the house in Hove.

Hove is fifty miles from London. The train journey from Victoria Station takes an hour. It had taken just as long for patients in South London to reach the Westbank Healing Sanctuary in Stamford Hill. Leah learned that the train journey made little difference to her patients in London.

As soon as the Healing Sanctuary in Hove opened, Leah was treating patients. Then Jack Doctors had a stroke of luck. An osteopathic practice close to Leah's healing sanctuary became vacant. Jack was able to sell his practice in London and to buy the one in Hove. The Doctors had got away to a good start in their new home, and as Leah showed her patients into her healing-room, she could reflect how much easier it now was to do her healing work. She had come a long way now from the first-floor flat in Bethune Road where she'd guiltily sneaked patients upstairs, warning them not to walk loudly, while she worried about her eviction order.

14

Dispersal of an Unsightly Growth

IN HOVE, LEAH Doctors worked freely, without landlord trouble and in pleasant seaside surroundings. And in Hove, healing work thrived even more than at Westbank.

For seventeen years, Mrs M Egan suffered pain and discomfort from fluid that leaked from her spine and settled in her right arm. Her arm and shoulder were enormously swollen. She looked deformed. She could use her arm only little, and only with great pain. She attended hospital for many years. Every doctor regretted there was no way known in medical science that could relieve her condition.

Mrs Egan was Irish and a good Catholic. She made a pilgrimage to Lourdes in France and prayed that God would cure her. She gained spiritual consolation that helped her resign herself to her condition.

But incessant pain was a goad. It drove Mrs Egan to Harley Street to consult a specialist. He confirmed what so many doctors had already told her: her complaint was incurable. She could obtain some relief if she attended hospital regularly to have the fluid drained off. It might help to reduce the enormous swelling.

For many years Mrs Egan was a hospital outpatient, having the fluid drained off. But draining only gave a few days' relief. Soon the swelling and pain returned and she was in agony once more. Although she was a Catholic, when acquaintances mentioned that spiritual healing could cure, she bought the *Psychic News*, read it, and decided to try it.

'I was feeling suicidal,' Mrs Egan confessed. 'I had been to doctors all over the country. I have even crossed to Ireland to get medical help. But I was always told the same thing: they said I was incurable.'

THE HEALING POWER

Mrs Egan telephoned Leah from London for an appointment at the Healing Sanctuary in Hove. When she arrived, Jack Doctors opened the door and, when she removed her coat, he was shocked. Her arm was swollen to frightening proportions. He told me: 'The swelling was so intense that below the armpits there was a solid mass of flesh that seemed to be fused to the body. It was impossible for Mrs Egan to wear a normal dress. She had to wear a frock with a deep, eight-inch patch in the sleeve which allowed room for her deformity.'

As soon as she laid hands upon Mrs Egan, Leah went into a trance. Through her, Dr Chang told the patient that her illness could be cured. He estimated that it would need three or four treatments with special healing rays. The first healing treatment lasted about thirty minutes, and Mrs Egan returned for two other healing sessions. She had this to say:* 'After three treatments from Mrs Doctors, the swelling went down. I was able to place my hand between my armpit and ribs, something which had been impossible for years. Up to then the flesh had literally stuck together, and was always sore.'

But Dr Chang had not yet concluded his healing. Mrs Egan also suffered from arthritis. Her right hand was useless, her fingers unable to move. The healing treatment continued for another three months. Every week the stiffness decreased in her fingers. Mrs Egan said:*

> Mrs Doctors is a wonderful woman. She has made all the difference to my life. Even the headaches that used to plague me have gone – and my nerves are better than they've been for years.
>
> I was due to go into hospital for some tests just before I saw the medium. Doctors had told me nothing could be done, but I felt I had to try. Thanks to healing, I was able to cancel my hospital visit.

Ten years after her healing rays treatment, in August 1972, Mrs Egan informed me in writing that she was cured.

* *Psychic News* Sept. 15, 1962.

15

A 'Spirit Operation' Disperses a Tumour

MRS LILY ARCHER had suffered chronic bronchitis for sixteen years and since the age of twenty-four had endured the pain of a benign stomach ulcer. Her chest condition was bad and did not respond satisfactorily to medical treatment. Her general health was so low that a proposed stomach operation had been postponed a number of times.

'I'd been taking pills and medicines for a long time without result,' Mrs Archer said. 'When it was clear the hospital doctors couldn't help me I took a friend's advice and tried spiritual healing. After all, I had nothing to lose. But that didn't do me any good either. Another friend then suggested I should try spiritual healing at a Spiritualist Church. Also no good. Then I tried other spiritual healers. But nothing helped me so I gave up hope in spiritual healing, too. I had to accept I'd go on being ill for the rest of my life. The doctors and nurses at the hospital were very good and did their best, but I had to make up my mind that this was something I had to live with.'

But Mrs Archer had a staunch friend who was convinced that spiritual healing can help the sick. Although Mrs Archer had had her fill of spiritual healers, she gave in to persuasion and agreed to try just once more.

Mrs Archer, accompanied by her friend, arrived at Leah's Healing Sanctuary. She was extremely low that day. She wheezed, had great difficulty in breathing, and her stomach tumour gave great pain.

'Mrs Doctors had no idea what was wrong with me because my illness hadn't been mentioned,' Mrs Archer stated. 'But as soon as I lay upon the healing-couch she said straight off what was wrong with me. Spiritual healers hadn't done me any good, so I hadn't much hope. But Mrs Doctors inspired me with hope. Suddenly I had confidence she could help me. No other spiritual healer came straight out like she did and said what was wrong with me.'

Leah laid her hands on her patient, and after a few minutes Dr Chang came through and spoke directly to Mrs Archer. She was bewildered because she didn't know about Dr Chang. Leah's eyes were closed and as Dr Chang described the 'spirit operation' he was performing, Leah's hands moved as though it was she who was performing the operation.

'Dr Chang said he could help me and would eventually heal me completely,' said Mrs Archer. 'The strange thing was, his words convinced me. I just *knew* I could be healed. There was a strange feeling inside me. Not exactly burning, but a very hot feeling. There was no pain; but it felt as though things were moving around inside me. It was a weird feeling. What I noticed most was the tumour growing numb. And I'd stopped wheezing, too; it wasn't such an effort to breathe.'

Dr Chang told Mrs Archer that her post-spirit-operation condition would be critical for a week. He said she needed frequent healing treatment and that during this crucial period he would visit her during her sleep-state to continue the healing. He told Mrs Archer that she would not need to return to the Healing Sanctuary. Her healing was permanent. But if she had any doubts she could always make another appointment with Mrs Doctors.

This is Mrs Archer's account of what happened following her spirit operation:

On 2nd May (the day after the spirit operation was performed) I felt well but very sleepy.

On 3rd May I was still sleepy but otherwise felt all right.

On 4th May I had a terrible attack of coughing and was awfully sick. I vomited a nasty, green phlegm. It made me feel shockingly weak and ill. I couldn't get out to do the shopping and I began to wonder if all this messing around with spiritual healers was making me worse. It was a very bad day and I dreaded going to bed because that was when I coughed most. But that night I slept very peacefully.

I felt a little better the following morning, 5th May. But I wasn't well by any means.

The 6th May was about the same. I felt very weak but I couldn't bear the thought of food. All I had all day was a few cups of tea.

On 7th May, I felt ever so much better. As soon as I awoke I could notice the change in me, just as though a terrible weight had been lifted off me. I was breathing easily and I had no pain at all in my stomach. The relief was so immense it made me feel joyful, and, although I was still weak, I felt energetic and wanted to do things.

By the next day, 8th May, I'd lost my weakness, too, I felt wonderful. I felt as though I'd been . . . remade!

Since then Mrs Archer has never been troubled by her chest or with stomach pains. She attended her hospital for a new series of tests and the hospital staff were astonished. All traces of her illnesses had vanished.

There was a sequel to this healing. Five years later, Mrs Archer decided to live in Canada. To become an immigrant she had to pass a medical examination. She felt fit and well. But because of her long history of illness, and her past hospital record, she dreaded that her medical examination might be unusually long and searching. It wasn't. She skimmed through the examination easily, and emigrated. But then, right out of the blue, her new way of life in Canada was abruptly overshadowed. A warty growth appeared on her right cheek and grew steadily. Worse, a second warty growth appeared on her other cheek. Her doctors were puzzled. They prescribed medicines and ointments. But the growths were persistent. They became enlarged and disfiguring. Mrs Archer was sent to hospital to receive medical attention. It is the way of hospitals everywhere that patients have difficulty learning the nature of their illness. Mrs Archer could make nothing of the medical terminology used to describe her condition. But one fact she understood very clearly: she was to enter hospital and have the growths cut out.

Mrs Archer was appalled. The growths were disfiguring and she wanted to be rid of them. But if surgery was performed she would be branded on her face for the rest of her life. She shuddered at the thought. She wrote to Leah Doctors, pouring out her misery and pleading for Dr Chang to give her absent healing, as he had years earlier.

Mrs Archer's letter went by air mail. Six days later the growth on her right cheek lost some of its angry verve. The next day the rowths on both cheeks were numb and insensitive to pain or touch. Then she described in her diary how the growth on her right cheek had broken up into little pieces. Four days later, all that was left of it was a small, healing scar. The growth on her left cheek was more persistent. It didn't break up into pieces until some days later. But within a month both growths had completely disappeared. Not a blemish remained to show where they had been.

Leah Doctors' records show that Dr Chang gave absent healing to Mrs Archer on the day Leah received her air-mail letter. It was the first day Mrs Archer noticed the initial change in the growths.

16

A Healing that Failed

NOT ALL PATIENTS of the Healing Sanctuary in Hove are being cured. One patient who was not healed is Mrs Howes, who travelled to Hove in the hope that she would benefit from Leah Doctors' spiritual healing.

In 1957 Mrs Howes had suffered from arthritis in the knee. Walking was difficult and painful. She saw an advertisement for the Doctors' Alliance Hall public healing demonstration* and attended it. She was one of the patients who limped up on to the platform and received osteopathic and spiritual healing from Jack Doctors. She told me she'd walked off the platform, quite healed. She had no further trouble with her knee until January 1972, when she fell and banged her knee, and once again it pained her severely. Once again she could only hobble.

More than fifteen years had elapsed since Jack Doctors had treated her. But Mrs Howes felt that he was the only person who could help her. She had a large cyst upon the knee and Jack Doctors suggested that Mrs Howes should make an appointment with Leah for spiritual healing. Mrs Howes made a blunt statement about herself which couldn't have been easy, but which made her feel a better person; it was the kind of statement few people would have the courage to put into words.

'I realise now I really wanted to go to Mrs Doctors so I could receive a message from my dead husband,' Mrs Howes told Jack. 'I'd had a terrible time with him for the last four years of his life. He was

* See page 41

impossible to live with. He changed so much. He wasn't at all like his real self. He used to be a kind, gentle, and affectionate man. But he began to change and finally I couldn't bear it. I got so desperate I made a terrible prayer. I prayed to God to take him from me. And God did! I learned afterwards he'd been suffering from cancer of the bladder, but he didn't know it because it didn't give him much pain. But it must have affected his nerves and made him how he was. If I'd known he was ill, I would have been more tolerant with him. But I didn't, and his behaviour killed all my love for him. I was eighteen when I first met him and we'd been together all these years. But the way he changed wiped out all we'd meant to each other.'

Later, while Mrs Howes was lying on Leah's healing-couch and Leah was laying her hands on the patient, she startled Mrs Howes when she said: 'Was your husband like this?' – and described him exactly the way he was. Mrs Howes had not told Leah or Jack Doctors what her husband looked like.

Mrs Howes said this about her meeting with Leah Doctors: 'I knew she must be talking about his spirit and I asked her: "Is he here? Can he see me?" Mrs Doctors said he was there and he wanted to give me a message: "He says he is very sorry. He wants you to forgive him. He couldn't help himself." I knew then there was a power at work which had brought me to Mrs Doctors. It was so that my husband could pass on this message to me; so I would know how he felt, and know how he could understand me, too. Tears came to my eyes. I didn't mind very much then when Mrs Doctors told me she didn't think Dr Chang could do very much for me, apart from giving me absent healing.'

But Dr Chang's absent healing didn't help Mrs Howes much either. 'Every evening at ten o'clock when I sit down and give myself up to the healing spirit, I can feel a warm glow all around my knees,' Mrs Howes continued, 'but it doesn't get much better. I still can't walk properly and it gives me a great deal of pain. I took my friend's advice and went to see some bone specialist at the hospital. Now I'm waiting to go into hospital to have an operation. They've got to remove some of the bone and fit a metal joint in its place. I'm not looking forward to it, but it's got to be done. It's so bad now I can't even walk. If it wasn't for kind friends I wouldn't be able to manage at all.'

Mrs Howes was born in 1898. When I investigated her case she was seventy-five years old.

I asked Dr Chang why he could do nothing for Mrs Howes. She was suffering and in need of assistance. It couldn't be she was resistant to spiritual healing because fifteen years earlier she'd received a combination of osteopathic and spiritual healing from Jack Doctors which had been effective. Dr Chang explained that, regrettably, he did not succeed in focusing his healing rays right into Mrs Howe's spirit. He was unable to penetrate right through into the patient's spirit; the healing rays failed to heal – as sometimes happens.

17

A Lenghty Healing

MRS KATE ROWLAND was thirty-four years old in 1961 and seriously ill. She had been injured by a medical instrument that had been inserted internally to correct a tilted uterus, and she was suffering the consequences of blood poisoning. Her body and her brain had been infected and, while undergoing emergency treatment in hospital, she was given drugs that had had serious side effects and caused a deterioration of her general condition. Mrs Rowland had lost all faith in hospitals.

'Over the months I became more and more ill, and it gradually became clear that the doctors and consultants could not undo what had been done,' Mrs Rowland described her plight. 'I was going steadily downhill. By 1968 I knew I was dying. I was able to eat only very little and I was warned to drink the minimum. Any fluids I drank were absorbed into my blood the wrong way. The doctors tried all ways to get me better, but nothing worked. They must have known, as I did, that I hadn't much longer to live.'

Mrs Rowland had previously tried spiritual healing without any improvement in her health. But since professional medical skill was unable to check her weakening condition, she decided she'd once more try spiritual healing. She had learned of Leah Doctors and made an appointment to see her. By then she was very weak. Her body was full of fluids it couldn't break down, and her vision was so blurred she had to be escorted everywhere. Her husband brought her to Leah Doctors' Healing Sanctuary in Hove.

The first healing session was in 1968. Dr Chang told Mrs Rowland he was confident he could restore her health; but only with long-drawn-out treatment; and the healing sessions had to be at least twice a week. This entailed many long journeys for Mrs Rowland and her husband, but they accepted Dr Chang's conditions unhesitatingly.

'To start with, I made two visits a week to Mrs Doctors,' Mrs Rowland said. 'Later on it was reduced to one visit a week. Apart from my body being full of water, it was also full of poison; because none of my glands functioned properly. Dr Chang told me he was keeping me alive while he cleared the poisons out of my body. After that he would give attention to my glands and get them working properly. I had innumerable spirit operations; Dr Chang explained they were necessary to keep my body functioning. I must have been a frightfully difficult patient. When I started receiving treatment I was in a terrible state. I couldn't do my housework or go anywhere by myself. I was in constant pain and since the poisons reached my brain I was dopey and couldn't think clearly. My eye-sight was affected, too. Everything was a blur. But after each healing session with Dr Chang my condition improved. Although I still don't have much energy I can get around now and do things I couldn't. I can do the shopping and housework, have evenings out with my husband, and go away visiting relatives. It's as though I'm beginning to live again.'

I spoke with Dr Chang about this case. He said he was very pleased with the progress, though it was only little by little. 'She is only three-quarters healed,' he told me in November 1972. 'The healing will still be long and wearisome for her. But she is responding to it well. Provided she continues the regular healing sessions, it will be possible to get her completely fit and well again.'

There is little doubt that Mrs Rowland will continue the healing sessions even though it might still be years before she is cured, because she has absolute faith in Dr Chang, and believes that continued healing will eventually free her from *all* traces of her complicated illness. And Dr Chang commented that 'her health will be gradually improving more and more – until she will be enjoying life again; and her enjoyment is already sweet because she had once resigned herself to death.'

18

A Mysterious Illness

THE FOLLOWING CASE shows how the healing work of Dr Chang and Leah Doctors not only benefits their patients but through them can help others who are sceptical about spiritual healing.

At the beginning of 1969, Mrs May Franklin developed symptoms that became progressively worse. She had increasingly frequent attacks of abdominal pains, and chronic diarrhoea. She lost her appetite, was continuously sick, and lost twenty-one pounds in weight within nine months. Her puzzled doctor became concerned at her condition and transferred her to the West Middlesex Hospital. Mrs Franklin was three times examined by physicians and surgeons. Her stomach, intestines and gall-bladder were X-rayed. Mrs Franklin was *not* told what the diagnosis was as a result of these examinations. She was given *no* treatment and was asked to return to the hospital in six months for another examination.

Six months is a long time to wait. Mrs Franklin continued to suffer the symptoms of her mysterious illness, and still lost weight. This energetic thirty-six-years-old lady became a weak, listless shadow of her previous self.

If the hospital specialists did not, or could not, recommend any treatment for her illness, what else could she do but wait out the six months? But Mrs Franklin knew instinctively she dare not wait the six months. She was growing continually weaker. She was withering away. It was a long journey to Hove, and she didn't feel she could face it. Instead, she wrote to Leah Doctors asking for absent healing.

Dr Chang started absent healing in December 1969. But he was not satisfied with the results. Mrs Franklin was a patient who needed additional psychic power that a medium can give to a spirit doctor. It was arranged that, despite the travelling difficulties, Mrs Franklin should attend Leah's Healing Sanctuary in Hove.

When she set off on her journey, Mrs Franklin was so weak she almost turned back, unable to face the train ride. It required will-power and resolve to keep the appointment. But when she lay upon the couch and felt the comfort of Leah's cool fingers, she was glad she'd made the effort. She felt a strange confidence that everything was going to be all right.

Dr Chang focused his healing rays upon her, using the psychic power that Leah could contribute, and told Mrs Franklin she would be healed. She would need more contact healing sessions, he told her, and prescribed a diet that would control her diarrhoea.

Mrs Franklin responded well to her first healing rays treatment and consequently required only one more healing session. One month after her first visit to Dr Chang in February 1970 all symptoms of her illness had disappeared and she was rapidly regaining her normal health and strength. A few weeks later she was back to her normal weight and seething with energy.

The sequel to all this occurred in the late spring of 1971. Mr Brian Franklin, who'd been greatly impressed by Dr Chang's healing of his wife, was concerned about the health of his friend's wife. Mrs P was suffering from a growth that had penetrated into the intestines and was causing an obstruction. Surgical intervention was needed. The diagnosis was ominous. If a growth obstructed the intestines it would have to be removed to save the patient's life. But if the growth *was* removed, and it was malignant, the growth would probably spread to other parts of the body. Surgeons often cut away cancerous growths successfully, if they are caught at an early stage. But when the cancer has a strong grip on its victim, essential surgery often activates new growths which in their turn require fresh surgical intervention.

Mr Franklin feared for the future of Mrs P. Before she underwent an operation which might have unpleasant results, he pleaded with her to try spiritual healing. He argued that she had nothing to lose, and if no good results were gained, Mrs P could still undergo the surgical operation. But Mr and Mrs P were practical people, concerned only with the hard realities of life. They would not 'dabble in a lot of spiritualist bosh'! So, in desperation, Mr Franklin wrote to Leah, pleading for absent healing for Mrs P. He regretted that circumstances obliged him to ask for it 'in this behind-their-backs fashion'.

Leah showed me a letter written to her by Mr Franklin, dated 8th July 1971:

> Dear Mrs Doctors,
>
> I think you would like to know that Mrs P . . . . . . is out of hospital. Her husband told me that the surgeons had expected to find that the growth had penetrated the intestines, and that they had anticipated having to remove part of them. The surgeon was surprised to see that the growth did not penetrate the intestines at all. He was able to peel it away.

Another letter from Mr Franklin, dated 25th July 1971, stated:

> Dear Mrs Doctors,
>
> I am very glad to be able to tell you that Mrs P . . . . . . is now well on the way to recovery. She will not have to attend hospital again. Her growth was either non-malignant, or was caught in time. Very many thanks for all your help.

Dr Chang began absent healing for Mrs P upon receipt of Mr Franklin's letter. There is *no* proof whatsoever that Dr Chang's treatment contributed in any way to the improvement in Mrs P's condition. It would have been invaluable if all the incidents described above had been enacted under the watchful eyes of a medical investigating committee. Especially interesting would have been a full medical report about the growth that was 'peeled away easily from the intestines'. Was this a *live* cancerous growth? Or a *benign* growth? If so, do reports of a growth 'peeling away easily' occur often in medical records?

19

A Patient's
Mental Attitude

MRS I U has asked me not to publish her name for personal reasons. She had suffered arthritis for eighteen years. Arthritis is an extremely painful and crippling disease. It attacks the joints. In its last stages the bones fuse together; the ball-and-socket joints become solid and immovable. And there is no cure for this disease. It sometimes runs its course swiftly and devastatingly, transforming a young person into a hunched cripple. More often it gains ascendancy very slowly, taking many years to transform agile fingers into a gnarled, claw-like hand. In the process the victims suffer acute pain from the swollen joints. Mrs I U was advised by her medical consultant to use warm wax upon her hands to ease the pain. When the pain was very acute he prescribed pain-relieving tablets.

Mrs I U had endured her pain for eighteen years and was resigned to suffering it for the rest of her life. She went on a holiday in 1971. As ladies do, she got into conversation with another guest on holiday in the same hotel. This is Mrs I U's personal account of this meeting:

She spoke to me the day before I was due to leave for home. When she learned I was in severe pain she told me she was a spiritual healer and would give me healing. I had severe pain in my legs and she gave me treatment for a short time. I was sitting beside the swimming-pool and she simply put her hands upon my legs and hands. It was uncanny. I had a weird tingling sensation as though something was passing through my body. Almost at once the pain in my legs seemed to ease. The thumb of my right hand had swollen up even more just recently and had become so bad I couldn't move anything with that hand. The pain was so bad my son had pleaded with me to ask for an operation in hospital to get rid of the swelling. But only a few minutes after she began healing treatment, the swelling began to go down. That was over a year ago and now I can play tennis and get a strong hold on my racket.

The spritual healer Mrs I U met was Leah Doctors, who had managed to get away for a very necessary and well-earned holiday. But she was too compassionate to forget her healing gifts.

Subsequent to her healing, Mrs I U visited Leah's Healing Sanctuary in Hove and received more treatment. Dr Chang diagnosed that she was also suffering arthritis of the hip. This was a condition he could only cure with frequent healing sessions over a long period. Mrs I U lived in Sheffield and her personal business made it difficult to make long, frequent journeys to Hove. The less effective absent healing was decided upon and is still being given.

Dr Chang told me that some patients respond well to absent healing. But other patients make slow progress without the psychic power that can be contributed by Leah's laying-on of hands. Absent healing without the direct physical involvement of Leah is sometimes beyond Dr Chang's ability.

Some medical consultants seeking an explanation of spiritual healing argue that apparent cures can result from a patient's mental attitude. If a patient is worried, and his nervous system is over-strained, it is not uncommon for aches and pains to develop in all parts of the body. Doctors know that a person's mental state influences his physical body.

Almost everyone has had personal experience of this. When we are badly frightened, it has an alarming effect upon us. Our hearts pound, our hair stands on end as though bristling, and our stomach feels that it is dropping away from us. In a theatre seat that is bolted firmly to the floor, while watching a cinema film on a wide-screen, we may experience physical sensations that are created entirely by our minds. A film that makes us a passenger on a fairground switchback can give us the bodily sensation of cresting a rise, and then hurtling down a steep slope. Our stomachs lurch sickeningly. Yet our physical body hasn't moved. Only our imagination has sat in that car and caused our bodies to feel the roller-coaster sensations. A shocking road accident frequently affects people so strongly that they not only feel sick, they *are* sick!

And, for years afterwards, simply recalling the accident makes them sick again.

Because their mental attitude can affect people so strongly, some doctors suggest that some illnesses are caused by the mind, and that patients get better by adopting a more healthy mental attitude. To express it briefly, many medical consultants believe some patients' aches and pains are caused by their mental attitude, and, if they are convinced by a Spiritual Healer that they will get better, they *do* get better.

Whatever the explanation of spiritual healing, the crucial proof of the pudding is in the eating. The important thing is that a patient should be cured. Therefore, when describing Leah's healing wotk I have frequently quoted the tape-recorder reports of patients about the progress of their illness. If it is argued that a patient's faith in a spiritual healer contributes to his healing, we must wonder why a sick person cannot have faith in medical consultants who have professional qualifications. Common sense should surely inspire *more* faith in a doctor than in a non-professional spiritual healer, who has no medical knowledge and may be a charlatan.

20

An 'Irreversible' Illness Reversed

IN 1963, Mrs G M Aitchison suffered abdominal pain and diarrhoea. Her local doctor recommended her to a hospital. She submitted to a thorough examination and was given a barium enema. Subsequently she was informed she was suffering from diverticulitis. The symptoms of this condition are that the walls of the intestines lose their elasticity and sag in folds. These folds form pockets in which undigested food can gather and putrify. The condition usually causes infection of the intestines as a side effect.

The treatment prescribed for Mrs Aitchison was a strict low-residual diet. She was to eat only foods which contain no roughage to be trapped within the intestines. This strict diet not only ruled out foods the patient enjoyed; it also ruled out many foods that contributed to the patient's general health. And the diet was not healing treatment. Mrs Aitchison was told by hospital doctors there was *no cure* for her condition. However, a strict diet would reduce its unpleasant symptoms to the minimum. She would have to persist with the diet for the rest of her life.

After eighteen months of this strict diet, Mrs Aitchison felt very low and depressed. But she was an intelligent and well-educated lady who possessed an MA degree and an open mind. She'd placed her faith in science and it could do nothing for her. She wondered if spiritual healing could do what medical science couldn't. She visited Leah Doctors. Afterwards she told me:

> Mrs Doctors examined me and said that if I visited her two or
> three times a week for three months she could guarantee I would

be cured within that time. I'm closely associated with the medical world so I was sceptical. But I complied with Mrs Doctors' conditions.

While I was receiving treatment I enquired about my physical condition and asked for Dr Chang to give me advice. He spoke to me through Mrs Doctors. Occasionally, while giving treatment, she would say: 'Dr Chang said so and so . . .' I would not have thought Mrs Doctors was 'entranced' at that time. She was always fully conscious and chatty in an ordinary way. I was even surprised that she never found it necessary to be silent while giving me healing treatment. Usually, I didn't feel any immediate relief – but usually found it a few hours later.

After a few weeks treatment with Mrs Doctors, some of my worst symptoms diminished. At the end of three months, almost to the day, I was free of all the symptoms of my illness and felt fit and well.

Three years later, in 1968, I spent three months abroad and picked up an intestinal infection, which failed to yield to medical treatment. When I returned to London I attended a well-known teaching hospital where my son was a medical student. I was thoroughly examined and underwent various tests, including a barium enema and a barium meal. The subsequent X-ray tests revealed no trace whatsoever of my previous diverticular condition. When I informed the radiologist that in 1963 I'd had a similar test and was found to be suffering from diverticulitis, he said that it did not show up in the X-rays, or was 'nominal' to the point of complete unimportance.

My son who was about to qualify showed me a section in one of his textbooks about diverticulitis. He said it confirmed that diverticulitis is what is know as 'irreversible'. The condition cannot be removed, nor altered by any known medical means.

Despite this, in 1963, the medical consultants and their X-rays confirmed that I was suffering from diverticulitis, whereas in 1968 the doctors and their X-rays could find no trace of this.

One possible explanation is that the 1963 diagnosis was incorrect. But if it was incorrect, it does not explain why I was suffering all the symptoms of this illness for almost two years; and it didn't begin to abate until I received healing treatment from Mrs Doctors.

Mrs Aitchison is a clear-thinking lady with the ability to adopt a detached objective viewpoint. She told me:

It seems to me that Leah Doctors' healing work is not limitless in its scope. For instance, she was never able to help me very much with the terrible pain of arthritis which I suffered when I lived in Brighton. She was willing to try; but I never got relief and healing from it as I did from the diverticulitis. I can't explain this; I am more than grateful for what she did do. I don't suppose Mrs Doctors herself could explain it either. Perhaps there is some reason why the pain of arthritis is difficult to remove in my case. As I've already told you, I don't understand *how* this healing works, but I always felt that Mrs Doctors knew what she was doing. Sometimes her hands felt very cold; at other times warm. When she dealt with infections, sore throats, and colds, her hands were icy cold. I think she works with an instinct. She knows – or is told by Dr Chang – what to do, and it worked for me, with the exception of my arthritic pains. Perhaps some kind of rapprochement is necessary between healer and patient for healing to be effective. In my diverticulitis case it undoubtedly was. I shall always be grateful.

As a Christian, I believe *all healing comes from God.*

When I first went to Mrs Doctors, who is Jewish as you know, she told me that when she was still young, she had a vision of Christ who came to her and told her that her life-work was to be healing; she already knew she had healing power. I believe she dedicated her gift in accordance with this vision and command. Not having a Christian background, she would not know she was in the Christian tradition, nor relate her healing to other healers who take their inspiration from the New Testament. But Christ also told his disciples who were distrustful of a man who was 'casting out evil spirits in His name' because he was not 'one of them', to 'rebuke him not, for he that is not against you is on your side'. I don't know what brought the Chinese element into the picture, except that many sages of both East and West must have known the laws of health and healing, and practised it in the Christ spirit of love, to greater or lesser extent.

I do not know anything about 'Dr Chang' except what Mrs Doctors herself says. He could be a thought-form of Mrs Doctors in which she ardently believes and which guides her. When one reaches this 'world of spirits' it behoves any Christian to be alert, as I believe there are such things as 'evil spirits'. Whether they are actual entities, or the projection of disordered and un-Christian-like thinking, who can say? Reading the New Testament, it is clear that in Christ's day, epilepsy, for instance, was clearly regarded as an unclean spirit which inhabited a person's body and could be cast out only by Christ's purity of spirit and love for the victim.

I therefore prefer to state that I received healing treatment from Mrs Doctors, who has faith in Dr Chang, rather than that I received it from Dr Chang, whom I do not know; though I must say the messages I got always seemed to be true and good sense. But I do not want to be associated with a Dr Chang cult, because healing is such a wide and diverse field, and I am very much against personality worship, and many people are intensely credulous. I prefer to put my faith in God – and all these various entities are mere channels of Healing.

* * *

Dr Chang made it clear to me on many occasions that he and his medium are mere instruments through whom God heals the sick. His and his medium's aim is to help sufferers regain their health, and, like Mrs Aitchison, he is decisively against any 'Dr Chang Cult' and personality worship, as he pointed out in the various interviews published in this book.

21

Leukaemia Cured

WHEN I ASKED Dr Chang which of his cures was the most successful, without realising it I was really asking which of his cures was the most sensational. His reply jolted me into considering spiritual healing from the human viewpoint, instead of with a journalistic slant. Dr Chang answered: 'Any time human suffering is alleviated, or brought to an end, we are successful in doing God's healing work.' But he sensed what I had truly meant to ask and added: 'Easing suffering does not merely help the patient. Healing is like a stone cast into a pond. The ripples spread out increasingly and the patient's changed condition influences all those around him. Suffering is not only endured by the patient. It deeply affects all those who love him.'

Dr Chang then recalled a case that showed how sickness and death bring suffering to many; and how healing spreads its power for good beyond the patient's orbit.

In 1954 Mr and Mrs Jackson had a son named Leonard – a healthy baby who grew into a vigorous little boy, full of mischief and playful zest. Children are tireless. They shout and jump all day, burning up enormous energy. Little Len seemed even more lively than most little boys of his age. But in the summer of 1957, when he was three years of age, Leonard began to lose his immense vitality. At first, his parents were not concerned. Little boys often exhaust themselves and need to rest, so they can spring to life again with renewed vigour. But little Len's unusual lassitude increased. He no longer ran out to play at every opportunity. He lost interest in things and was now constantly physically tired. When Leonard's little face began to take on a puffy appearance, his parents became alarmed.

Their doctor didn't reassure them. He advised them to take Leonard to hospital at once. The worried parents pressed him for his opinion. The doctor said he didn't like the child's symptoms. There was a possibility that Leonard might be gravely ill. His condition justified immediate hospitalisation.

At the hospital the anxious parents waited tortured hours while Leonard was thoroughly examined and submitted to tests. The doctors called in a specialist. The long hours of waiting were ended by a medically confirmed dread diagnosis. Little Leonard had leukaemia. Cancer of the blood. The cancer had gained a powerful hold in the spinal fluid. Little Leonard Jackson was given a maximum of six weeks to live.

All parents can sympathise with the agony of Mr and Mrs Jackson. The event was too awful to contemplate. Their little boy, who had been so full of life and joy, was to be taken from them so soon.

The Jacksons wouldn't believe what the doctors had told them. Frantically they searched for other opinions and a different diagnosis. They took Leonard to the Hospital for Sick Children in London. There they waited and prayed there had been a mistake somewhere and little Leonard was not as sick as was thought.

Their hopes were smashed. Despite the sympathy of the doctors there was only one diagnosis they could give: advanced leukaemia!

The stricken parents were given tablets which the child had to take daily. An appointment was made for him to be examined by the hospital at a later date. There was nothing more the doctors could do.

Time was running out swiftly. Leonard now had only three weeks to live. Every day he was paler and weaker. His face grew more puffy, a visible confirmation of the doctors' diagnosis.

At such anguished moments, loving parents will do anything to save their child. They will willingly strip themselves of all their possessions, and eagerly surrender up their own lives. When friends urged the Jacksons to visit Leah Doctors it was a ray of hope they grasped frantically.

At the first healing session Leah went immediately into a trance and Dr Chang spoke to the parents. 'It is advanced leukaemia,' he confirmed. 'It is sited in the spinal fluid'. Dr Chang then described how he was focusing spiritual power healing rays upon the diseased area. He said that the child was showing excellent response to his treatment and he could cure him. But it would require a long and extensive treatment. He could cure Leonard only if healing treatment was maintained as he directed.

The parents felt a stirring of hope. Not only Dr Chang's words, but his confidence too, convinced them it was within his ability to cure little Leonard. They eagerly agreed to bring the boy for treatment as often as required.

Dr Chang's first treatment lasted half an hour. Almost all this time his healing rays were in full use. He told the parents to visit him again within three days. He said the child had responded well to treatment but although an improvement was already taking place, it would not be immediately evident.

Within two days Leonard seemed somewhat better. 'Our prayers for a miracle to happen have been answered,' Mrs Jackson told her husband. 'Let us pray this miraculous improvement is continued and our prayers answered,' agreed Mr Jackson. 'But let's hope, too, that we're not being tricked by false hopes.'

At the second healing session Dr Chang said the little boy had reacted even better than he had anticipated. And he told the parents that their boy responded so well to that day's treatment that they would see a considerable improvement. He said they would both be greatly relieved mentally to watch him regaining strength and energy. He said that when they took Leonard to hospital for his next appointment the doctors would be astonished at his blood count.

The parents were profuse in their thanks.

'Don't thank me,' said Dr Chang. 'Thank God. *All* healing comes from God. I am only the instrument.'

Leonard Jackson's condition noticeably improved in the next two days. He was much less lethargic, colour came back to his cheeks, and the puffiness of his face diminished. At the hospital the parents waited anxiously while Leonard's blood count was taken.

The result was what Dr Chang had predicted. The doctors were astonished. But wisely, they did not encourage the Jacksons to be too optimistic. A sudden improvement in the condition of a patient suffering from blood cancer is not unknown. It is almost always followed by a relapse. It would have been cruel to raise false hopes and at a later date have to give the parents bad news.

But Mr and Mrs Jackson were beginning to believe a miracle could occur. They took little Leonard again and again for healing treatment by Dr Chang. At the end of another fortnight, the spirit doctor said there was such excellent response to his healing rays that in future they need bring Leonard only once a week. Six weeks after the little boy's first visit, Dr Chang reduced healing treatment to once a fortnight.

There was no doubt little Leonard was recovering his health. He was lively again, had lost his wan appearance and puffiness around his face, and was full of energy. His parents began to believe their prayers for a miracle to happen had been answered. But the doctors at the hospital Leonard attended were still cautious. They agreed that the child seemed greatly improved, but warned the parents not to build up too high hopes. Again and again they had seen leukaemia victims improve in health for a time, only to relapse swiftly.

Mr and Mrs Jackson discussed this possibility with Dr Chang during the seventh week of Leonard's healing treatment. Dr Chang reassured them that their little boy would be cured and that the cure would be lasting. But the healing rays treatment would have to continue for some considerable time. To avoid a recurrence of his illness he had to receive the healing rays until every trace of cancer had been eliminated.

Weeks and months passed. Summer came around again and little Leonard was so fit and well that his parents asked the hospital doctors if Leonard could go back to school at the end of the summer holiday. The doctors said he could. They had been amazed at Leonard's astonishing improvement. They had regularly taken his blood count and were now able to say their tests showed no trace of leukaemia.

In the doctors' rest-room there were many discussions about Leonard Jackson. Many references were made to his inexplicable recovery. The word 'miracle' was used. And before Leonard began school again in the autumn of 1959, he once again underwent a searching hospital examination. He was declared completely free from leukaemia and Mrs Jackson was told there was no reason to continue visiting the hospital unless Leonard showed signs of a recurrence of his previous condition.

Leonard Jackson went through school without any serious illness and later found employment as an apprentice in an engineering firm. This involved heavy manual labour, moving machinery around. Later in life he decided to emigrate, submitted himself to the stringent medical examination required, and now lives in good health abroad.

'When Dr Chang said shortly before Christmas 1959 that *our Len was cured for ever,* I couldn't find the right words to thank him for having saved my boy's life,' Mrs Jackson told me. 'It was the best Christmas present any one could ever have given us.'

22

Eyesight Restored

ANOTHER CASE DR Chang mentioned was one which had special significance to me. I could sympathise with this patient more than most other people. I have never been completely blind. But I have lived on the threshold of that terrible condition.

Charles Preston was blind. He'd been told that medical skill and science could do nothing to restore his vision. He would remain completely blind for the rest of his life.

Charles was a printer by trade and thirty-four years of age when he heard this bad news. The tragedy of a sightless lifetime stretched before him.

'I'd suffered from weak eyesight from childhood,' Charles reported. 'As a schoolboy I had to wear glasses and was under the care of University College Hospital, London. Later I was transferred to the Western Ophthalmic Hospital. I had strong myopia, complicated by acute *glaucoma macula.*'

This is a condition that involves the centre of the retina. It affects the detail in the centre of the visual field. The fluid within the eyeball builds up pressure and when it is acute, only urgent medical attention can sometimes preserve the sight. Charles Preston suffered an overall deterioration of both eyes. Despite all that the ophthalmic surgeons could do, they finally had to tell him he would be blind for the rest of his life.

When a young and vigorous man is doomed to darkness, life becomes so difficult and full of such bitter memories that suicidal ideas are never far from the consciousness. We all feel deeply for those unfortunate people who are born blind. But the plight of the young and healthy who become blind is much worse. Those who have never seen cannot regret not seeing the beauty of a setting sun brushing the green fields with gold, or the grey-green sea dashing against white cliffs, exploding into surging foam and spray. The man who becomes blind must resign himself to many limitations. He cannot get around, his food must be cut up, he is constantly in peril of injuring himself, and the problem of earning a living is acute. Charles was tempted to finish it all; but he resisted temptation. He had the willpower to resist the easy way out of an unbearable situation. And he had a wife who was devoted to him. Her self-sacrifice and cheerful encouragement strengthened his resolve to grapple with life and overcome his handicap.

The only trade he knew was that of a master printer; but such work was now out of the question. Good eyesight is the first necessity of a printer. He had to learn a new trade suitable for blind people. He attended a school for the blind, overcame his handicap, and was employed in a workshop for the blind.

But he never completely abandoned the hope that he would recover his eye-sight. He visited many eye specialists, constantly hoping one might succeed where others had failed. And time and again he left a consulting-room with yet one more slim hope dispelled. Everywhere the story was the same: nothing could be done. He was blind for life.

Charles was a staunch Catholic. This religion teaches that if there is any communication with spirits it can take place only through a priest. Preston believed it wrong for anybody else to communicate directly with the spirit world. So when a well-meaning friend suggested spiritual healing might help, Preston at once spurned the idea.

But, unknown to Charles, his wife Elizabeth faced a serious problem. In 1958, her health gave way. She suffered acute stomach pains, lost her appetite and lost weight rapidly. Her nerves were so frayed that she had to maintain a tight control over herself to avoid breaking down. She attributed this to the worry of her husband's blindness. She had to keep cheerful and give him every encouragement, yet conceal from him the mental strain she suffered. Her condition deteriorated so rapidly that she feared her neighbours might comment to Charles in conversation how ill she looked. She consulted her doctor. He was worried by her symptoms and sent her to hospital. After examinations and tests, she was told she had cancer of the stomach, X-rays indicated that the disease was far advanced. An operation was necessary.

'I was told that the operation was not a guarantee that my health would be restored,' Elizabeth said. 'Although the doctors did not say so, I knew I was really being told I was slowly on my way to the grave. I couldn't tell Charles about it. He had enough troubles on his plate. I was afraid of what he might do if he learned my depressing news. I felt desperate. Then I remembered that a neighbour had suggested spiritual healing to Charles. I asked her to tell me more about it. She told me about Mrs Doctors and I made an appointment to see her at her Healing Sanctuary.'

During this healing, Dr Chang took over from Leah and spoke directly to Mrs Preston. He said she responded very well to his healing rays which reached her spirit satisfactorily. He said he could cure her and gave details of how the cure would be effected.

'He told me that within a few days the cancer would break up and would pass out of my body through my bowels,' Mrs Preston recalled. 'When the healing session ended, Mrs Doctors confirmed that I would be cured. I did already feel better. I was convinced I would get much better still. I know it sounds silly saying I felt better only after half an hour with Mrs Doctors. But don't put this down to auto-suggestion. All the time I'd been ill I'd been using autosuggestion, refusing to give way to illness, and convincing myself my willpower could overcome my disease.'

Three days after her first healing session with Dr Chang, Mrs Preston noticed the physical changes that Dr Chang had predicted.

'The cancer passed through my body and out through my bowels. I know this is fantastic and sounds like wishful thinking. You probably suspect I'm an easily impressed and gullible person. But I assure you I am not. I am always very sceptical about supernatural incidents that are supposed to have happened. But nobody has to take my word for it, anyway. It's all in the hospital records. I had an appointment at the hospital ten days after Dr Chang's treatment. They were expecting to operate on me and gave me more tests. I could tell they were surprised when they examined me even more thoroughly. Then the consultant specialist admitted he was pleasantly surprised; he couldn't find any trace of my cancer. They wouldn't operate, he said. They'd wait and see what progress I made. I could see he was puzzled. But the atmosphere of a hospital is so coldly clinical that I'd have felt a fool telling him my cancer had been cured by a spirit doctor.'

Relieved of her worry about her own physical condition made Mrs

Preston wonder if her husband could benefit as she had benefited. His flat refusal to 'meddle with spiritual healing' was understandable, for he was a very devout Catholic. But Elizabeth could do more than just persuade him. She could back up her arguments with her own first-hand experience, and the hospital records. She could show she had been due to have a cancer operation, but the need for the operation had disappeared. She timidly suggested spiritual healing to her husband.

'He was furious. He called me all kinds of names. He said I could sin if I chose but that was no reason why he should become a sinner. In one way it was ridiculous for us to argue. I was begging him to try the healing rays treatment that might cure his blindness. And Charles, who desperately wanted to be cured, put up every form of resistance. But I wouldn't give up. For his own sake, I kept on at him. He began to see that with all my heart and soul I really did believe that his eyesight could be restored. Finally, very reluctantly, he agreed I could make an appointment for him with Mrs Doctors.'

Charles Preston's first healing session took place in a strained atmosphere. Charles's conscience was not clear. He had consulted a priest and had asked bluntly if seeking spiritual healing was a sin. Father O'Grady, like all priests, had seen many men tortured by mental conflict, impelled to do things against their religious belief. He had every sympathy with Charles Preston. Who could condemn a man for his fervent wish to have his vision restored? The priest chose his words carefully when he answered. He confirmed that spiritual communication should only take place through a priest. But he explained the reasons for this. They were similar to the reasons of the General Medical Council. The public must be protected against charlatans and quacks. If no restrictions were imposed, many unscrupulous people would set up in the lucrative business of quack healing, extracting money from patients and giving nothing in return but unqualified and ineffective 'treatment'. The Roman Catholic Church had ruled that spiritual treatment must come only from a priest so that it could be assured that any spiritual healing that took place came from God, and not from an evil entity. The priest then provided Charles Preston with a loophole for his conscience. He said it was natural and proper for Charles to seek help to restore his eyesight; if he sought spiritual healing it was essential that he was quite sure it was *God's* healing.

So when Charles Preston submitted himself to the cool caress of Leah Doctors' fingers, he was on guard against everything. He had been warned that evil entities can be communed with. But after only a few minutes his uneasiness vanished. He had no sense of evilness or danger; only a peaceful serenity as though soothed by a calming presence. He knew an inner conviction that all would be well.

When Dr Chang took over and Leah Doctors spoke to him as a spirit doctor, it all seemed quite normal. Dr Chang explained his healing rays and told him his eyes were in a very bad state. It would take a long time to heal them completely. But he responded well and if he came for treatment regularly, the healing rays would benefit him enormously. Even after his first treatment he'd be able to see a little.

This seemed to Charles Preston a very sweeping statement. He didn't know how much his wife had told Mrs Doctors about his condition. He tested Dr Chang, wondering if the spirit doctor would change his attitude. 'I've been examined by many highly skilled, famous ophthalmic surgeons,' Charles said. 'They've all told me the same: there's nothing medical skill and science can do for me. They say I'll remain blind for the rest of my life.'

Dr Chang was unperturbed. He said he knew the surgeons could do nothing for him. Preston's vision could not be restored by medical science at its present stage of development. But the spiritual power healing rays *could* cure him. Dr Chang reminded Preston that all spiritual healing comes from God. Did not Jesus Christ often prove it?

'If it is God's Will then I am prepared to be healed,' answered Charles Preston.

At the end of his first healing session Charles experienced what he called a 'miracle'. Leah removed her fingers from his closed eyelids and when he opened his eyes – he could see!

He couldn't say his sight was restored. But he had lived a long time in a world of total blindness and now the blindness was shot through with lighter tones, and greys. The lighter greys were closer to the window. When the greys moved he could distinguish their movements.

'Your vision will return only gradually,' Dr Chang warned him. 'It will improve with every treatment. If you persist with the treatment, your vision will become increasingly clearer until you can distinguish objects distinctly.'

Preston didn't answer because tears were running down his cheeks and choked his voice. When he wanted to express his gratefulness, Dr Chang said as always: 'Don't thank me, I am only a humble instrument of God. Thank God. God can do *anything!*'

Charles Preston did thank God. On his way home he went to church, knelt, and thanked God for the great healing he had received.

Thereafter, Charles visited Leah Doctors' Healing Sanctuary every three days for more healing with a clearer conscience. After every treatment his eyesight improved. He was soon able to distinguish objects close to him, although the outlines were blurred. After the tenth treatment he was able to read large print. If he used a magnifying-glass he was able to read quite small print.

Charles continued healing treatment for eight months. At the end of 1958, he reported his vision to be much better than he had ever known it at any time in his life. But it was not perfect. He visited the Western Ophthalmic Hospital to have reading glasses prescribed. It was necessary for him to produce his medical card showing the medical history of his eyesight. The ophthalmologist was astonished. In all his experience he had never known a case of a patient with such a serious eye condition regaining his ability to see. If he hadn't been presented with Preston's full medical history he would not have believed such a recovery possible. Marvelling, he tested Preston for reading glasses, and soon afterwards, Charles was employed again as a master printer.

The ophthalmologist was so astonished by Preston's remarkable recovery of vision that he asked Charles to permit other ophthalmic surgeons to examine him. Charles did so willingly. The doctors were amazed and baffled. Preston's case was unique. They went into his medical history and made copious notes. They sought the medical explanation of his eyesight recovery, so that they could use the same treatment upon other patients.

At his next healing session with Dr Chang, Charles told him about the opthalmologists' astonishment.

'They'll be even more astonished as time passes,' Dr Chang told him. 'Your eyes will get stronger, your vision will improve, and the strength of your spectacle lenses will need to be decreased. But it will take a long time. You must have patience.'

Charles Preston continued Dr Chang's treatment and by mid-1960 his spectacles needed a lens of only 4·5 diopter for his right eye and 4·0 diopter for his left eye.

At the end of the year Charles Preston was offered an extremely good job overseas. It provided excellent opportunities for advancement. But by now he was so reluctant to abandon Dr Chang's spiritual healing as he had once opposed it. At the back of his mind was the nagging fear that without regular healing rays treatment he might go blind again. He asked Dr Chang what he should do. Dr Chang said his eyes were not yet as good as he wanted them to be. To give him normal vision, the ability to see without glasses, would require long healing rays treatment. Perhaps another two, three, or even more years. But because of the treatment he'd received up till then, his eyesight was healthy and strong. His eyes were cured of all disease but continued treatment with the healing rays would enable him eventually to abandon spectacles and have perfect vision. If he decided not to continue with the healing rays treatment he would always need his glasses for work. But he need have no fear that his sight would deteriorate without prolonged healing rays treatment.

'What do you advise, Dr Chang?' Charles asked. 'This job overseas offers excellent prospects. Shall I take it? Or shall Elizabeth and I stay here?'

'I cannot advise you,' said Dr Chang. He pointed out that everyone must make their own decisions in life. But he added that if Charles did go overseas, he would periodically visit him during his sleep-state, and watch over his eyesight.

Charles Preston, his wife Elizabeth, their daughter of one-and-a-half years, and their three-month-old baby boy underwent medical examination and emigrated. The X-ray tests of Elizabeth Preston showed her to be free of any trace of cancer.

Twelve years later, in 1972, when I last heard, the Preston family were happy and prosperous overseas. They had added two children to their family. Elizabeth Preston was in very good health. There was not the slightest sign of her cancer recurring. Charles Preston was working happily, still wearing spectacles with the same strength of lenses as those prescribed for him before he left the United Kingdom.

Neither Charles nor Elizabeth Preston have any doubts that the spiritual healing they received came, as Dr Chang insisted, from God.

23

Healing on Television

IN NOVEMBER 1965, Leah Doctors' Healing Sanctuary in Hove became the centre of unusual activity. Two large BBC television vans drew up outside 47 Goldstone Villas, thick cables coiled like snakes across the pavement and in through the front door, cameras were trundled around, and brisk young men talked loudly, using technical jargon. The neighbours watching all this activity could deduce from the vans that a BBC television programme was being filmed.

The prime mover in all this activity was Mr David Rea, director of BBC's television programme *Whicker's World*. It resulted from a decision to dedicate one of Alan Whicker's programmes to 'Fringe Medicine'. Many kinds of non-professional healing methods were suggested for this programme, including spiritual healing. Since Leah Doctors' spiritual healing work was well-known, not only through grateful patients but also through Press reports, Leah was suggested for inclusion in the programme.

Although the BBC operates independently, it is a government organisation. Its Charter forbids it to sponsor advertising. It also imposes many restrictions to ensure that the BBC does not offend public opinion, nor good taste. Programmes dealing with controversial subjects are often so ringed around with do's and don'ts that the producers seem to be walking on eggshells. The slightest slip can cause a storm of protest in the Press, and questions in Parliament. The wonder is that the BBC comes under criticism so rarely.

Mr David Rea wanted to present an interesting programme about fringe medicine. But it had to be produced with a skill and deftness that followed BBC policy. He had to be on guard against a charge of 'advertising'. So before he introduced Leah Doctors into his programme, he wanted to assure himself there was reasonable evidence that she was what she claimed to be: a spiritual healer who could heal. Through Leah Doctors, Dr Chang agreed to meet David Rea. He also confirmed he would be willing to demonstrate the effectiveness of his healing rays on television. Dr Chang favours the spread of knowledge about spiritual healing so that sick people will know that it can be beneficial.

David Rea visited Leah Doctors' Healing Sanctuary in Hove by appointment, and a patient agreed he could watch her undergoing healing treatment. The patient was Mrs Grace Steele, and this was her first visit to Dr Chang. David Rea watched her compose herself upon the healing-couch and saw Leah lay hands upon her and go into a trance. Dr Chang spoke through Leah, diagnosing the patient's condition. He said Mrs Steele had a serious heart condition. Two of her heart valves were narrowing and would soon cause serious deterioration in the patient's health. He said a spirit operation was necessary to open up the heart valves.

After this diagnosis, Mrs Steele confirmed it was what she had already been told by her medical consultant. She asked Dr Chang if he could help her and he said he'd perform a spirit operation. Mrs Steele was willing. She said her doctor had warned her she could pass away at any time. Without medical intervention she could not expect to live more than a few months.

Dr Chang 'operated'. He described every step of the spirit operation while he did so. Using his spirit instruments, he opened up the heart valves until blood flowed through them easily. David Rea watched.

Mrs Steele also suffered thrombosis in the leg. This had caused an unsightly dark brown lump to form, some four inches long. After telling his patient her heart condition was so much improved she could be confident it would give her no more trouble for at least ten years, Dr Chang turned his attention to the lump on her leg. Even as Mr Rea watched, the lump diminished in size and then disappeared.

David Rea had seen enough to convince him that Leah Doctors sincerely believed in her spiritual healing, and discussed with her the proposed television programme. He planned to bring his ten-man camera and sound crew to Hove to capture the true atmosphere of the modest Healing Sanctuary. It was suggested Leah should demonstrate a spirit operation being performed by Dr Chang. It was also arranged that five of her previous patients who had been declared medically incurable, should be interviewed about their condition *after* receiving healing treatment from Dr Chang.

The patient who volunteered to undergo a spirit operation on television was Mrs Gladys Wells. She was sixty years old and suffering from hiatus hernia. She was under medical care and had been told that only a surgical operation could put her right. She was registered at a hospital where the surgeon had recommended that she should undergo an operation. Because of her age, and natural wish to avoid painful surgery, Mrs Wells was anxious to try out a painless spirit operation. She had no objection to the spirit operation being performed publicly.

Among Leah's patients willing to be interviewed on television, was Mr Goodman. He had suffered for many years from Ménières Disease. This is a disease of the ear and its labyrinth. It causes recurrent attacks of vertigo, vomiting, and tinnitus, and often causes progressive deafness. Mr Goodman often felt giddy, the world around him swayed, and he lost his balance. He also suffered from a continuous ringing and buzzing in his ear. When examined at hospital he was told successful surgery *might* dispose of the noises in his head; his loss of balance could be cured, but almost certainly only at the cost of his hearing. He faced an unpleasant choice: to carry on living and enduring giddiness and a buzzing head; or gamble his hearing on the success of a surgical operation. He had become Dr Chang's patient, had undergone a spirit operation, and no longer suffered loss of balance nor ringing in his ear. His doctor said he was 'inexplicably cured' of his illness. Mr Goodman was willing to appear on television and tell how Dr Chang had cured him.

So was a lady who does not wish her name to be published. She was semi-blind when she came to Dr Chang; she had advanced cataracts in both eyes. Leah placed her fingers upon the lady's closed eyelids and at the end of the healing session, the cataracts had disappeared. Her ophthalmologist was astonished when he tested her eyes and found them healed.

A third patient was a lady who had suffered thrombosis before she consulted Leah Doctors. Her condition was so acute that her doctor warned her she could not look forward to a long life. After two healing treatments with Dr Chang, all her symptoms of thrombosis disappeared, a fact confirmed by her doctor. He added that 'inexplicable cures do sometimes occur.'

The fourth patient was a deaf lady when she'd first visited Leah seven weeks earlier. When Leah placed her hands upon this lady's ears, she experienced the same burning sensation that other patients had described. The burning was caused by Dr Chang's spirit instrument and his healing rays. After the treatment she could hear perfectly. She was ready to demonstrate this on television by repeating words whispered by somebody many yards away. This, despite the fact that her doctor and specialist had told her her hearing could never be restored.

The fifth patient was a woman with a bad heart. She'd been warned at the hospital that she hadn't long to live. Three months before the programme Dr Chang had performed a spirit operation upon her. Since then, her hospital consultant confirmed that all the symptoms of her heart condition had disappeared.

One spirit operation and five patients to interview meant a long day's filming for the BBC television unit. Alan Whicker and the television crew watched Dr Chang perform his spirit operation on Mrs Wells' hiatus hernia. When Dr Chang learned that, although this spirit operation was being filmed in November 1965, it would not be screened on television until January 1966, some ten weeks later, he pointed out that this long time-lag would enable Mrs Wells to feel the *full* benefit of the healing, and report upon it.

After the spirit operation, the five patients previously mentioned were interviewed by Alan Whicker. He asked searching questions and the patients produced evidence of their previous illnesses. They then demonstrated they were now quite free of the illness which had been considered incurable. All the members of the BBC unit were very impressed by what they saw.

Before the programme *Whicker's World – Fringe Medicine* appeared on the television screens, doctors were consulted about Mrs Wells's medical condition after the spirit operation. They confirmed that all traces of her hiatus hernia had disappeared. Enquiries were also made about the medical condition of the other five patients who had been interviewed. In each case it was confirmed that they had been very sick people before they visited Leah Doctors, and free from all their symptoms of ill-health after treatment by Dr Chang.

But there was a slight disappointment for Leah when she eventually watched herself on the television screen. The television unit had spent most of a day at her healing sanctuary and had material for an elaborate programme. But all this material had to be drastically cut and condensed into a scheduled time-limit for the programme. Although Dr Chang's spirit operation on Mrs Wells was shown to the public, Alan Whicker's interview with Leah Doctors and Dr Chang was abbreviated. And there was no time at all to televise any of the interviewed volunteer patients.

The programme was televised a second time on BBC1 in February 1968. Before the screening of the programme it was confirmed that Mrs Wells was still free of her hiatus hernia. It was also confirmed that the other five patients had experienced no recurrence of their illnesses since Dr Chang's healing.

Many viewers became interested in spiritual healing, many written enquiries were received by the BBC and it was decided that the public interest warranted another programme about healing. This time it was to be in colour. So, in January 1972, Leah Doctors' healing Sanctuary at Hove was once again invaded by television cameras. The programme this time was for the *Man Alive* series, whose director was Harry Weisbloom. Dr Chang performed another spirit operation.

The patient was Mr Harold Slater. He had received a blow upon his thigh-bone which had caused his left leg to become swollen and inflamed. His doctor and a hospital consultant diagnosed the condition as phlebitis. The treatment prescribed was absolute rest in bed for three to six months. Meanwhile, pain was to be subdued by the controlled use of prescribed drugs.

After Mr Slater had got upon the healing-couch, he was asked how he felt. He said he was in pain despite the pain-relieving drugs he had taken. Without the drugs, he suffered excruciatingly.

A little dramatic touch was included in this televised spirit operation. Measurements were made of Mr Slater's swollen leg, and recorded before Leah went into a trance. Dr Chang took over and performed a spirit operation, maintaining a running commentary on his work and chatting to the patient. Mr Slater, with great relief, reported that the pain in his leg was diminishing. At the end of the spirit operation, he declared he was quite free of pain. When Mr Slater's leg was measured again, its swelling had decreased by half-an-inch.

This spirit operation was followed by an interview with Leah Doctors and Dr Chang; and Mr Slater was asked to return to the healing sanctuary three weeks later. When he kept his appointment, all swelling had disappeared from his leg and both his doctor and the hospital consultant had confirmed that he no longer suffered from phlebitis.

This filming of a spirit operation was televised in the *Man Alive* series under the title 'If the Spirit is Willing' on 8th March 1972. At that time Mr Harold Slater was in the best of health and quite healed. This was the third television screening featuring Leah Doctors and Dr Chang, and the estimated number of viewers was twenty-six million.

Dr Chang and Leah were rewarded for their healing tenacity. All over Britain new hope was raised in many sick people who had never dared to hope again until they'd seen these programmes. Many more patients visited Leah's Healing Sanctuary in Hove, and dozens of letters arrived daily asking for absent healing.

Throughout the United Kingdom, among the healthy as well as the sick, there is a growing feeling that perhaps it is possible that spiritual healing really can *heal!*

24

A Healer Seeks Healing

MR SIMON STARK of Folkestone is a spiritual healer. He specialises in treating mentally handicapped babies. He has been very successful in his healing work. He not only treats mentally defective children, he also trains the parents to give spiritual healing to their children themselves.

In February 1966, Mr Stark was suffering so badly from rheumatism that his back had become completely rigid. It was acutely painful. After one healing session with Leah Doctors he was able to touch his toes and move around freely, and was relieved of all pain.

Although he is a spiritual healer himself, Mr Stark pays great tribute to the considerable and valuable healing of medical practitioners and consultants. In February 1965, he had no hesitation in undergoing a surgical operation in St Bartholomew's Hospital, London. The surgeon performed an operation for hernia. Afterwards he told his patient that the peritoneum, the thin membrane which lines the inside the abdomen, was 'like an old sack'. There was every probability that Mr Stark would have to return for another operation within a year.

Unhappily, the surgeon's pessimism was justified. Another rupture appeared just before Mr Stark visited Leah Doctors for his rheumatic back. It was only natural that he should consult her about this second hernia. Dr Chang said he would help him.

'Leah just stroked over the hernia,' Mr Stark told me. 'But there was an immediate dramatic improvement like there'd been with my rheumatism. So I had no doubts. However, forty-eight hours later, I was sitting in my fireside chair reading the newspaper when I suddenly felt as though I had an elastic girdle tightening around my abdomen. I panicked for a moment. I thought: "What's going to happen?" I had the feeling that my intestines were being lifted, and some pain inside, exactly like the pain I'd experienced on my other side after my surgical operation at St Bartholomew's. After that I took it easy with my manual work for a couple of weeks. But all signs of my hernia had completely disappeared. Now, in 1972, if I lift something heavy, I sometimes get a warning pain in my right side, the side operated upon surgically. But the side operated on spiritually is much stronger.'

Mr Stark underwent another spirit operation in 1968. Because of an emergency he was racing up the stairs of an old house. The ceiling was very low and he gave his head a smashing blow on an old beam. After his dizziness had subsided, he was in great pain. He made a digital exploration and concluded that he had cracked two of his neck vertebrae. This would mean wearing a plastic neck-collar for many weeks while the bones healed. To avoid this, Mr Stark prayed for his own healing guide to help him. But his guide specialised in handicapped children. So Mr Stark wrote to Leah Doctors and asked for absent healing.

'Within forty-eight hours I was aroused at about 1.30 am by a voice whispering: "I have come to attend to you, my son." It was Dr Chang,' Mr Stark told me. 'I answered him, half-asleep: "Thank you, doctor. Please go ahead while I drift back to sleep".'

The morning after, Mr Stark was pain-free and sure that the bones in his neck were knitting. Two weeks later he felt completely healed and he has never been troubled by his neck since.

* * *

Mr Stark recommends all patients whom he cannot help himself to contact Leah Doctors. One of them was his uncle, Mr Elias Stark, who had come over from Capetown on a visit.

Mr Elias Stark was eighty-six years of age in 1966. His sight was so bad he could only watch television if the brightness was turned full on, and if he was within eighteen inches of the screen. His hearing was so defective that he heard sound as very faint and garbled. While he was in Britain he had a bad attack of constipation and was warned by doctors that he might not survive the long journey back to Capetown.

Elias Stark had consulted many South African specialists about his bad sight and hearing, and also about his chronic constipation. They'd prescribed many and varied remedies. One had been a strict diet that partly comprised cooked seaweed. Mr Simon Stark made an appointment for his uncle to visit Dr Chang.

'Dr Chang first concentrated upon my Uncle's vision,' Mr Stark informed me. 'Afterwards, he told him to wash his eyes out twice a day with cold water. He said calcified dead blood-cells would permeate out through the cornea and had to be washed away. He also directed his healing rays upon my Uncle's ears and body.

'Two days after visiting Dr Chang, my Uncle could watch television from a distance of six feet with normal brightness,' continued Mr Stark. 'He could hear without any difficulty and his bowels were functioning normally. Today, at ninety-two, my Uncle can read my typing and he writes to me in his own hand-writing. Previously I had to write to him with a thick felt-pen using letters half an inch tall. He is in perfect health. He had also asked Dr Chang to try to increase his life-span so that he could complete a project he was engaged upon. Now that he has finished this project, he is prepared and content to pass on.'

* * *

Mr Stark also told me about the unusual case of a woman visitor from Canada. This lady was suffering such a severe attack of migraine that Mr Stark telephoned Leah Doctors and asked for urgent absent healing. Within an hour, the woman's pain had disappeared. She was very impressed and said everyone *must* learn that spiritual healing works. But when Mr Stark took her at her word and suggested using her name as a witness to the effectiveness of spiritual healing, 'she became most unpleasant – I would not advise that details of her case be published. She might sue for damages.'

25

Dr Chang's World

LEAH DOCTORS IS a modest person. It is a sad fact that many people, caught in the limelight, or finding themselves possessed of a special gift, become overbearing and self-important. Vanity is a human failing that is extremely difficult to overcome. But Leah Doctors has never believed herself anything other than a humble means by which spiritual healing powers can be conveyed to those who need them most. She is happy simply being an instrument to help ease human suffering.

Dr Chang is equally humble. Although on occasions he confidently asserts that he can heal a patient, he always makes it quite clear that, like Leah, he is only the instrument through which God can focus the spiritual power healing rays upon the sick.

Neither Dr Chang nor Leah Doctors make any claim to being 'unique'. Nor do they wish to be considered so. They are of minor importance, they believe. What *is* important to them is that healing shall be successful through their mediumship.

Any book about Dr Chang and Leah Doctors should not highlight *them*, they insist, but their *healing*. Our world is preoccupied with materialism and science. But awareness is gradually spreading that when and if it is sought, evidence of supernatural powers can be found.

* * *

I had many interviews with Dr Chang in 1972 and 1973, quizzing him about the spirit world in which he lives, and his healing rays. To chat with a spirit was a strange role for me to play. I was a down-to-earth, hard-bitten journalist. I sat opposite Leah who relaxed on a settee with her eyes closed and answered my questions in a soft, slightly sing-song voice that wasn't her own. She spoke with the voice of Dr Chang, the spirit of a Chinese doctor who had died five hundred years earlier.

I needed the gentle hum of my tape-recorder to remind me I was living in the material world of the twentieth century, and not in a mystical fairyland.

I had my pencil in my hand and my notepad upon my knees. But as I scribbled notes I reminded myself that when I first visited this house, it was as a man threatened again with rapidly deteriorating vision. I could not now doubt that I could read what I wrote. This had been brought about by the mediumship of Leah Doctors, and the healing rays of Dr Chang.

I asked Dr Chang a thousand questions. But for the benefit of readers I have selected only the most interesting ones. I have also condensed the questions and answers.

I detected Dr Chang's uncertainty about his ability to heal some patients and asked him if he knows immediately after examining a patient, if it is possible to affect a cure or not? Dr Chang explained:

When I first examine a patient, I can't tell if the treatment will result in a cure. I simply don't know. I first make a test to see how the patient reacts. After a patient has been 'bathed' in our healing rays we have some idea how he is likely to respond to treatment. But then, we often can't be completely sure. We often have to wait a few days to see how the patient progresses. Sometimes, we still don't know after a number of healing rays treatments if we can cure a patient or not. In such cases there is little we can do except leave it all in God's hands. Whenever we fail to tell a patient we can cure him, it is because we don't know if we can. Sometimes miracles happen. We ourselves don't know *why* miracles come about.

In conversation with some of Dr Chang's patients they'd described incidents which indicate that Dr Chang has an awareness of the future. I asked him if he did indeed have clairvoyant awareness of the future. I asked if he could see a patient's future, and, if this was the case, he surely knew whether a patient could be cured or not.

'I can't *always* foretell the future,' Dr Chang said. 'But *sometimes* I can. It's the way it happens. Sometimes I *can* see ahead; but sometimes, even if I want, it is *impossible.'*

I asked if he could change the destiny of patients. If a patient were dying, and Dr Chang helped him recover and thereby helped him to avoid death, would he have changed his destiny?

Dr Chang answered that whenever *Karma** has destined a person to die, nothing can avert his death.

I asked: 'Is it right to say you *can't* help a patient who is suffering excruciating pain from a fatal illness if *Karma* rules that he or she *must* suffer?' Dr Chang's reply was:

> It is very difficult to explain this to you, *Sometimes* we *can change the Karma;* whereas on many occasions we can do nothing whatsoever to change it. We ourselves don't know why this is so. We have had cases where a patient has got better, whereas his *Karma* ruled that he should not have got better. In some cases *Karma* ruled that a person *must* pass away; yet we have managed to prolong his life on earth for another few years, perhaps to enable him to make certain important provisions that otherwise would not have been possible. Sometimes we have a patient who, *Karma* rules, *must* pass away – but at this moment his family may be very dependent upon him and in great need of his help. Perhaps this is the reason he is allowed to live a little longer – so that he can help others. You can see that this is a very difficult question for us to answer, since we ourselves don't know *why* these things happen.

I asked Dr Chang why patients suffering from the same illness don't respond to his healing rays treatment or spirit operations in the same way. Why was one patient's eyesight healed after two or three healing sessions, while another patient, with the same eye trouble, needed healing sessions lasting weeks, months, or years? The reply was:

> The reason why one patient with a certain disease is cured by me, while other patients with exactly the same disease *aren't* cured, is because our healing rays are not received in the same way. It is essential that our healing rays penetrate into the patient's spirit and spirit body. If the healing rays do not penetrate deeply into the spirit we cannot cure. This applies to all patients; those

---

* The word *Karma* is used by Buddhists. It means, roughly, the sum of a person's experiences, plus, and combined with, his destiny. In everyday language he was saying that nobody can escape their predeterminated experiences.

attending for contact healing here at Leah's Healing Sanctuary, and those receiving absent healing. With absent healing we have to get around to help people.

I have often seen with some patients that our healing rays penetrate straight through to their spirit and spirit body. Whenever this happens we can be sure their health will greatly improve overnight. But with others our healing rays cannot penetrate deeply enough. When we fail to focus them upon their spirit sufficiently effectively, their condition improves only slightly. To be fully effective our healing rays *must* reach the spirit very deeply. And when I say spirit I don't mean the mind. I mean the *inner spirit*. Then they *can* be cured. But if they have great faith, and yet the healing rays cannot penetrate to their spirit, then they cannot be healed quickly.

Psychologists and medical science accept that simple faith can help people greatly, even enabling them to make a swift recovery from a serious illness. I asked Dr Chang if it was essential for his patients to have strong faith in him, and faith that he can cure them. I asked if he can cure people who are sceptical and have *no* faith whatsoever in his healing ability. Behind my question was a personal interest. I had first come to Dr Chang without faith in him and had been very critical of his healing powers. Dr Chang:

The only important thing is that a person *comes* to me to receive spiritual healing. What they believe is unimportant. My patients are of many religions. Many come to me without faith that I can heal them. They are desperate and despairing, regarding me as their last resort. But it doesn't make the slightest difference whether they believe in spiritual healing or not. But it *is essential* that they must sincerely *long* to get better. If they sincerely wish to be cured, then this frame of mind greatly helps their healing. If we then are able to penetrate deeply enough to reach their spirit, we can heal them, and it is quite unimportant if they disbelieve in spiritual healing. It isn't the *mind* of a patient that is important; but penetrating right into the spirit is essential. We have had patients who assert they don't believe in God. But our healing rays penetrated through to their spirit and they have got better. It is not belief in spiritual healing that is important. It is our ability to be able to reach through to the spirit that is important.

It might interest you to know that quite a number of confirmed Spiritualists, with absolute faith in spiritual healing, have consulted us, suffering from all kinds of illnesses. Yet we were unable to cure some of them because we couldn't reach right through to their spirit. Faith and belief are not enough. It helps. But it can only help when the healing rays penetrate fully to the patient's spirit and cure him that way.

If a cat or dog is ill and Leah lays hands upon them, the animal will heal quickly, because we can penetrate an animal's spirit very swiftly. Animals do not have a barrier surrounding their spirit. Humans *do have* a barrier. Sometimes it is strongly-built and very resistant to spiritual healing. Nearly all human beings have this barrier, which we on this side can see.

In many cases when people are gravely ill, they 'cling' to their illness. This strengthens their barrier. Without the patient realising it, he is clinging to his illness, and doesn't want to relinquish it. In such cases it is often quite impossible to separate the spirit body from the physical body and our healing rays and spirit operations cannot be effective.

I asked Dr Chang to differentiate between the spirit and the spirit body.

DR CHANG: The spirit and the spirit body are two separate things . . . But they are very closely linked. To cure, we must reach right through to the spirit. When Leah lays on her hands, we are able to penetrate the physical body and then work on until we reach the spirit through the spirit body.

HUTTON: You start with the physical body? Then you penetrate through to the spirit body? And finally you reach the spirit?

DR CHANG: Exactly.

HUTTON: Spirit body and spirit?

DR CHANG: Yes.

HUTTON: These are three separate things? The physical body, the spirit body, and the spirit?

DR CHANG: That's right.

I knew Dr Chang had achieved many healing successes and I wondered if he was willing to co-operate with qualified registered doctors. Dr Chang said he would be delighted to discuss with any doctor his patients' illnesses.

HUTTON: But it is a fact, isn't it, Dr Chang, that you have no present-day medical qualification? You do *not* practise orthodox medicine? In these days of highly-developed medical techniques you would have difficulty in understanding what a present-day qualified medical specialist was talking about?

DR CHANG: It doesn't matter in the slightest about the correct use of medical terms. That's unimportant. What counts is that we *can cure* patients. in many cases we can cure patients who have been declared incurable by medicos. I cannot give you an *exact* explanation and description of our healing rays. But anybody can understand a symbolic description of how they work. We spirit doctors have our own methods of healing which are quite different from those used by human doctors. But both methods can be linked and we can work in harmony to reduce suffering. We'll welcome any, and every, opportunity to work with your earthly doctors.

Dr Chang did not think his claim to cure patients who have been declared incurable by medical specialists would cause friction between orthodox doctors and himself. Spirit doctors, and human doctors, he said, have a common cause: to cure the sick. The methods used shouldn't be important; but the successful healing of a patient should please them both. Again he emphasised he very often can be no more sure than an earthly doctor that he can restore health to a patient. He could only be certain that his healing rays would cure when he *knew* they were reaching deep down into the patient's spirit.

DR CHANG: When I'm uncertain I will only say that I will do my best. Nobody can say more than that. But sometimes it can be more specific. We had one patient, Mr Alfred Stevens, who lived in Hampstead.* He had a tumour on the brain. After the first application of our healing rays I *knew* that I could remove the tumour in about two weeks. I could see how the rays were penetrating deeply into his spirit and were influencing the tumour, reducing its size. I told Mr Stevens to persist in treatment because I knew I could cure him. He did. His tumour broke up and disappeared. Today he is fit and well.

I asked Dr Chang about those sad cases where it was clear to him that his healing rays and spirit operations would be of little avail.

DR CHANG: In hopeless cases it is usually wiser not to tell the

* His first healing session was in November 1964.

patient. I recall Mrs Alice O'Connor who made a long journey to visit Leah for healing sessions. After her first visit I knew Mrs O'Connor couldn't live long on this earth. There was nothing we could do to prevent her from passing over. But we didn't tell her this. Instead, we comforted her and eased her pain. While she did live, she was not, therefore, completely bedridden. She could get up, sit in a chair, talk to friends and be happy with their companionship. The illness was in her brain. We knew she had only a short time to live. We didn't mention this. But we are not sure if it would have been better to warn her husband. Quite often one cannot be sure what is the right thing to do. And sometimes we know we make mistakes. But if we were wrong in not giving a warning, we can at least be comforted that Mrs O'Connor's last days on earth were peaceful.

Drug addiction is so widespread it has become a disturbing medical problem. A high proportion of drug addicts are young people. Alcohol addiction is also a form of drug addiction. But its slow poisoning of the body and its relentless damaging of vital organs are so insiduous its victims usually die of an illness indirectly brought about by alcohol poisoning. Fatalities that can be directly attributed to alcohol are rare. But hard drugs carry their victims straight to the grave. Once hooked on hard drugs, the victim is doomed. The drugtaker's body adapts to the regular intake of the drug until the bodily organs are entirely dependent upon it. The victim literally cannot continue to live *without* a minimum dosage of the drug. This is why drug-addicts are registered and are granted a legal prescription of drugs. They must be saved from dying for lack of it. Yet, paradoxically, the regular intake of the drug also leads to the grave. But more slowly. The hard drugs the drug addict's body needs to keep life going relentlessly eat away the health and mind of their victim within a few short years. When hooked on hard drugs, unless he is helped at a very early stage of the addiction, the victim is beyond human help.

I asked Dr Chang if drug addicts were beyond spiritual healing help as well?

DR CHANG: We *can* help drug-addicts. But it is very, very difficult. They must come for treatment when we tell them; and they must be persistent and return again and again. It's a very lengthy treatment. But unfortunately drug-addicts tend to be irresponsible. They are unable to persevere. We heal them by drawing the poisons out of their body. With long treatment we can eventually clear their system of all the effects of the drug. But a great deal depends upon their attitude. We do all we can to help them by assisting them to relax. If we can soothe their nerves, and ease the craving after we have extracted a quantity of drugs from their bodies, then we can slowly rid them of their desire to take more hard drugs. But healing drug-addiction is very difficult. The patient must visit us often and sincerely wish to be cured.

All healing is basically a restoration of normal health and vigour to an affected part of the body. A diseased lung can be treated until the tissue is no longer invaded by infection. But some bodily organs can become so seriously diseased that they no longer function. Many victims of kidney disease have only one functioning kidney. If this also ceases to do its work, they cannot live. I asked Dr Chang if it is possible for him and his fellow spirit doctors to regrow, or renew, diseased organs or tissues? His reply was interesting:

I can never foretell what I can do for a patient until I have first seen how deeply my healing rays can penetrate to reach the spirit. I am always very careful not to make unjustified claims. I can't help somebody by saying I can do something which I cannot. It depends upon the patient; and every patient is an individual case. The deciding factor is how deeply my healing rays can penetrate.

I have a patient, Miss Linda Robinson, who visited me after she had undergone a surgical operation on her spine. The hospital surgeon had cut away a part of her body. The operation was unsuccessful and when the lady visited me she was suffering constant agony. Our healing rays could reach very deeply into her spirit and we knew we could cure her. But to do so we needed a 'spirit pad' to replace what had been cut away. There is no better way I can describe this to you except as a 'spirit pad'. We placed all this 'pad' upon the lady's spine and immediately she was relieved of all pain. In a way, this is what you would regard as regrowth. We saw what the patient needed to heal her, we manufactured a 'spirit substance' to replace what needed replacing, and she was free from pain; we had restored her to good health.*

If you think about it, when we cure leukaemia we are also

* Miss Robinson first visited Leah Doctors in 1963. To this day she has never had any return of her spinal trouble.

using regrowth. The blood cells of the body are defective; our healing rays renew them.

Our healing rays are of enormous assistance to us. With them we can even heal a part of an eye that is severely damaged. With them we can heal diabetes, cancer, heart diseases, and many other killer diseases.

We would like to have many more of these serious cases brought to us. Many patients are declared medically incurable, yet if we have the opportunity, we could give help to those who have abandoned hope much more often.

I asked Dr Chang if after treating a patient for whatever illness, he ever felt confident enough to guarantee that the healing had been completely successful and that the trouble would never recur?

DR CHANG: No. That we cannot guarantee.

Dr Chang explained that he very rarely felt he could guarantee the future health of a patient, any more than an earthly doctor can do so. He could feel overwhelmingly confident; but he could never guarantee complete recovery. There is an element of uncertainty in his spirit world, it seems, just as in our world.

I talked to Dr Chang about his failures and he confessed them frankly.

As I've told you, there *are* cases when I *cannot* heal a patient because we cannot reach the patient's spirit sufficiently. But often we also fail because the patients come for *one* healing session expecting a miracle. If they are not miraculously transformed into healthy persons after one visit they conclude we are not helping them and don't return for more healing treatments. They wouldn't expect their own doctor to cure them instantly. Indeed, many patients spend weeks and months visiting doctors and hospitals without losing confidence in their medical consultants. But very often, some patients I know I can cure after a series of treatments, don't return after their first healing session. It's only rarely I can cure a patient on the first visit. And I can't always tell at that time how many other visits may be required. It varies greatly. Some patients can be cured with three, five, or ten visits, whereas others may need treatment lasting many months.

Absent healing is impeded even more by patients breaking off contact. Frequently, when an absent healing patient feels better, he decides he's improving and stops writing to us. When the link between us is stretched until it snaps in this way, the partial benefit of our healing that the patient has already enjoyed can suffer a relapse. The patient thinks he had only imagined he was getting better. Some of these patients tell friends they tried absent healing and it failed to work. Sadly, these words reach the ears of other sick people who might have sought our help if they had not been discouraged in this way.

I tried to encourage Dr Chang to discuss how those in the spirit world could help us on earth in ways other than healing. But Dr Chang was clearly disinclined to discuss human affairs which didn't directly involve spiritual healing. He specialises in healing and isn't to be drawn into other activity.

He agreed with me that drug-addiction is a terrible fate. He said that he and his spirit helpers were always ready to give any takers of drugs every co-operation to help free them from the vice. But, when I suggested that he and his helpers could also help by suggesting ways to prevent the spread of dangerous hard drugs, he became vague, like a layman confronted with complicated machinery he doesn't understand, yet knows it is dangerous to tamper with it.

'We help all we can by healing people,' said Dr Chang. 'It is not part of our work to meddle with preventing drug-trafficking. Many people think we can do this and that, as though we have miraculous powers. But there are laws and ways, and things that alter and fashion events. All these things must be understood fully to be able to deal with them. Suffering is appalling. Who could *not* want to stop wars if it was within his power to do so? But I am a spirit doctor, a healer. There is nothing I can do to stop wars; nor drug-trafficking.'

I asked Dr Chang what impression he had formed as a result of being in contact with the earth through Leah Doctors?

DR CHANG: I have to say that at the present time your world is in a very bad state. It is always very depressing for me when I know I have to come here. Every time I visit you I feel I must weep. You people have completely abandoned the basic religion, which is *'Help thy neighbour - Love thy neighbour'*. And yet it could all so easily be so different. All it needs is for people to adopt a basic religion of goodwill and help each other, instead of fighting each other. If everybody were to love and help their neighbours, they could live as though in heaven. There would be no trouble in your world. Yet all around I see strife and gloom. It's because *everybody, everywhere,* wants *everything* their way. It's so evident that *all* people can't have *all* their own way. Yet they obstinately persist in trying to get it. It causes war between nations, and misery in small family and social groups.

HUTTON: In this book I am writing about you I would like to convey a message from you to its readers; and to the world.

DR CHANG: I have a message; a very short one but a vitally important one: *People everywhere must help each other.* That's my message to the world.

26

A Grim Warning

BEFORE BEGINNING TO write this book, I made it clear to Dr Chang, as I have to readers, that I have no intention of being a propagandist for Leah Doctors and Dr Chang. I began my investigation with a genuine desire to discover the true facts about their spiritual healing. And I have been able to report some cures that seem remarkable.

But healing treatment of this kind is fraught with danger if patients do not take normal, reasonable precautions. I would be guilty of grave neglect if I failed to warn readers that blind acceptance of spiritual healing can bring them great distress. I would not be alive today to issue this warning if I had blindly depended upon spiritual healing. As I will explain later, absolute faith in spiritual healing could have led me to my grave.

My investigations show that practising spiritual healers can be classified in three categories. No qualification, or licence of any kind, is required for a person who decides to practice as a healer. There is no law to prevent anybody buying advertising space and therein describing himself as a healer and soliciting consultations and offering absent healing. In practice, magazines publishing such advertisements usually discriminate. They will not accept adverts from a new healer unless some clear evidence is provided that healings have been performed by the advertiser. But, for an unscrupulous charlatan, fabrication of such evidence presents little difficulty.

Thus, I place in my first category of healers those who are unmitigated rogues. Their sole objective is to fleece the sick and maim. They cold-bloodedly exploit adversity, and if their patient's 'faith' is strong, they wring every penny from it. These frauds are plausible and convincing. Their skill is in acting out the role of a healer; and often an unscrupulous trickster-actor, who has studied his 'healer'-part, plays it better than a genuine healer. 'Healers' of this type are a serious menace to society. Their victims can suffer a disastrous decline in health as a result of consulting them. But they cannot be exposed until an official inquiry is made into spiritual healing. Genuine healers will welcome such an investigation; they have, in fact, been pleading for one for years. But meanwhile, these tricksters can endanger life with impunity and the public ought to realise how dangerous they can be!

The second category of healers are good-intentioned men and women. They are eager to benefit mankind and seek no personal gain. But they lack the healing powers they believe they possess. They are dominated by a state of mind that may spring from excessive religious zeal, or their longing to help mankind. They may even on occasions possess some small degree of healing power. But basically, they are self-deluded. They believe they are what they are not. This is a common human failing. Most people at some time believe themselves to be more capable than they are. And a man who is convinced he can heal cannot be condemned for wishing to help mankind. Nevertheless, good intentions can often have tragic consequences.

The third class of spiritual healers are genuine. Spiritual healing is brought about by their mediumship, and an examination of their case histories shows it. Leah Doctors' place is in this category. I have reported a great number of healings brought about through her mediumship and the evidence I have has been checked, and these healings have persisted over twenty years. Nevertheless, even with genuine spiritual healers, grave dangers confront any patient in a critical state of health who has such absolute faith in the healer that he does not even consider seeking medical advice.

It must be remembered that the medium is a tool. Dr Chang stated clearly that healing power comes from God, or Mother Nature, which is the Ultimate Power. Leah Doctors is merely an instrument through which this healing power is conveyed to the patient.

Leah Doctors has never claimed to be other than an ordinary woman who is happy to be used for a worthy purpose. She is of flesh and blood; a human being. Like all human beings she has her failings. For twenty years she has worked with Dr Chang, most of the time controlled by him and speaking in his voice; obeying his wishes and instructions almost by instinct. It would not be surprising if such close working harmony with Dr Chang has blurred her sensitivity at the borders of her contact with him; not surprising if at times she asserts *herself*, instead of Dr Chang. And I believe this happened when Leah Doctors nearly sent me to my death!

Leah is a natural, cheerful, impulsive woman who knows her healing is guided by Dr Chang. But after twenty years of working with him closely, I suspect that unless she analyses herself *all* the time, there are occasions when she fails to distinguish between Dr Chang's guidance and her own impulsive diagnosis. It is not done deliberately, I am convinced. Leah Doctors is not aware when personality is superimposed upon Dr Chang's guidance.

The human frailty of a medium is an ever-present risk, and a reason why *all* who consult spiritual healers must take sensible precautions. They should *always* obtain qualified medical opinion and be guided by it. They should *never* place *absolute* faith in a spiritual healer only, never fail to consult a qualified doctor, and never fail to heed a doctor's advice.

When this book was almost written in 1973, I became disturbed about an ugly swelling under my left armpit. I visited my doctor who asked me to see a consultant surgeon. The specialist said I must undergo a surgical operation to remove a tumour. Owing to the shortage of hospital beds, the earliest date that could be fixed was nearly three weeks away.

I dread operations and pinned my hopes on Dr Chang. I was still receiving healing rays treatment for my eyes and decided to discuss my arm trouble with him at my next healing session which was a few days after my visit to the surgeon. We talked, as usual, during the treatment, which lasted some time, and then Dr Chang said: 'That's finished for today.' I sensed he prepared to leave. 'Just one more thing, Dr Chang,' I said quickly.

I could not see Leah Doctors, who was standing behind me. I therefore do not know if she was still controlled by Dr Chang. Nevertheless, I described my arm trouble. Leah placed her hands upon my shoulders for some minutes and then told me my trouble was 'nothing serious', that the cause of it was 'acid', and that I'd soon be all right.

Luckily for me, I was unconvinced. Leah had spoken in her normal voice, she did not give a clean-cut diagnosis of my complaint as I felt sure Dr Chang would have done, and her vague reference to acid seemed to me to be stupid, especially as I already knew the surgeon's diagnosis. I felt let down by Leah.

I believe that if I'd received Dr Chang's healing rays treatment during the following three weeks, I could have been an excellent guinea-pig test case for a special spiritual healing success or failure. I could have observed what happened to the large and ever-expanding swelling under my arm. But it was dismissed as acid, I was told it was nothing serious, and discouraged from persisting with spiritual healing.

If I had had blind faith in spiritual healing, believed that my trouble was just acid, and that it was 'nothing serious', I would have died.

If I had delayed even a fortnight in undergoing my operation, there would have been no hope for me. As it was, the tumour was just operable and could be excised. For weeks after I was critically ill and even while writing these words, I am still on prescribed drugs, and months away from restored health.

This statement is not a denunciation of Leah Doctors. As long as mediums are human, such lapses are inevitable. A medium who has spent many hours on her feet, healing one patient after another, cannot fail to suffer fatigue. And at such times the rapport between spirit guide and medium may dissolve without the medium being aware of it. I am quite sure Leah is a useful and valuable tool for Dr Chang. But I am equally sure that fatigue and familiarity with Dr Chang's routines have their effect. She does perhaps not always realise when he is no longer with her. She must also have a strong impulse to speak as Dr Chang, when he is needed, yet is unable to respond. I think this occurred when Leah Doctors made herself ridiculous to millions of *News of the World* readers.

Michael Litchfield of the *News of the World,* quite fairly, took up Leah Doctors' advertised offer to perform spirit operations. He visited her for a spirit operation. He had had his appendix removed twenty-seven years earlier but paid Leah £2 to have it removed by a spirit operation. It was a completely fair test of Leah Doctors' claim to diagnose illnesses. Leah failed the test and treated Michael Litchfield for his non-existent appendix.

It is regrettable that Leah Doctors merited unfavourable publicity in the *News of the World* with this 'boob', because it may offset recognition of the valuable healing work she has done.

But I would not claim that a similar boob could not occur again. As long as mediums are human instruments there is always the risk of a human failing. In similar circumstances, Leah could again wishfully think herself into contact with Dr Chang.

It can happen to all honest and genuine mediums. That is why I end this chapter by repeating my warning: Nobody should place absolute, blind faith in a healer!

A qualified doctor should always be consulted, his opinion respected, and his treatment adopted.

27

Investigate Spiritual Healing!

FROM A SMALL house in a small town, Mrs Leah Doctors and Dr Chang have provided extremely impressive circumstantial evidence that spiritual healing gives results. The healings described in this book are not scientifically proved facts of healing. This is so because most of these healings had taken effect before attention was drawn to them. Not many people want to bother with non-medical individuals who say they can cure cancer. But if cancer is dramatically healed, then the healing excites great interest. Yet since the healing wasn't supervised by specialists step by step, doubt is aroused about the spiritual healer. Perhaps the patient didn't have cancer to begin with? A mistaken diagnosis in the first place is how a spiritual healer's successes are often described. The doctors who scoff at spiritual healing often argue that there's no satisfying proof that spiritual healing takes place. They overlook that General Medical Council regulations prevent spiritual healing from being investigated scientifically.

In my own case I *know*, as only a man who has been near blind *can* know, that my sight was very considerably improved by Dr Chang through Leah Doctors' mediumship. But my simple statement is not acceptable as scientific proof; nor would be most of Dr Chang's healings.

Dr Chang points out: 'What is important is that people shall be healed. Once they have been healed, they can get along very nicely without a signed statement by scientists that they were cured.'

That their spiritual healing has not been put to scientific test is not the fault of Dr Chang, or Leah Doctors. They have never shirked submitting their spiritual healing rays and spirit operations to scientific investigation. On the contrary, Leah has many times striven to have Dr Chang's healings and cures investigated by specialists; men whose judgement cannot be refuted because they command respect.

Such an investigation would require very little effort from investigators if they are men who genuinely wish to discover the truth.

Any large hospital could co-operate in such an investigation without disturbing its normal routine. Six patients suffering from an incurable disease could be accepted as volunteer patients for spiritual healing. Their full medical records would already be on file, giving the full history of their illness, and the date when their medical consultants decided that medical science could do no more for them. These medical reports could be made available to investigators so that they could confirm for themselves that the condition of the volunteer patient was indeed medically incurable.

If any, or all, of these sick patients improved their condition, or were completely cured, the investigators could then consider if enough evidence of spiritual healing has been provided to justify a serious and profound investigation of Dr Chang's healing.

If there were no change in the condition of the patients, the investigators could declare it publicly, and make it quite clear, that spiritual healing has not proved anything.

Common sense urges that failure to hold such a simple investigation is anti-social. If spiritual healing could be packed in cans and sold over the counter, a hundred wealthy canning combines would be competing and researching spiritual healing.

There are many spritual healers. The degree of their healing successes varies. But there are some who have provided seemingly impressive 'evidence' of spiritual healing. Yet if there were only one, and if this one *could* demonstrate mediocre successes with spiritual healing, common sense demands that even these mediocre healings should be investigated to the full. Anything that can add to man's knowledge of healing is not to be lightly dismissed!

There can be no two ways. Either spiritual healing works; or it doesn't! If it doesn't, then those who practise it are a menace to society. They raise false hopes, and delude the public. Their shabby victimisation of the sick should be exposed publicly. Their 'healing cures' should be officially declared to be fraudulent claims.

If spiritual healing is a delusion, a scientific investigation would expose it. Nobody has anything to fear from such an investigation except the fraudulent or deluded spiritual healers.

But if such an investigation proved that spiritual healing occurs, either in explicable or inexplicable ways, then man's knowledge would have been immeasurably increased. A new field of study would have been opened up for research and exploitation – for the benefit of the present and future generations.

To heal the sick is a great, human task. If spiritual healing works, then co-operation between spiritual healers and medical practitioners and consultants might revolutionise medicine. Mankind might be relieved of a great deal of its pain and suffering; and a new standard of health and strength, never before envisaged, might be achieved.

If spiritual healing does work, the only barrier to harmonious co-operation between doctors and spiritual healers is a few man-made regulations. These laws were drawn up for the purpose of protecting the public. It was never intended that they should deprive people of a great benefit.

After my conversations with Dr Chang and Leah Doctors I know that their wish is to help heal the sick. Rules and regulations prevent their healing as widely as they know they can. I have come to share their belief, despite the dangerous blunder Leah made when she diagnosed my tumour as 'just acid' and 'nothing dangerous'. I am convinced that a scientific investigation of spiritual healing could result only in the good to the community. The public should be *encouraged* to seek spiritual healing if an investigation established that it worked, or *stringently warned* not to rely on it if it was proved useless.

Dr Chang and Leah Doctors want doctors, nurses, and spiritual healers to work together in harmony, increasing their power to heal the sick.

EPILOGUE
by
Dr Michael F Kirkman

Dedicated to Mr William P Lawrence

'IN THE BEGINNING was the Word and the Word was God.'

'In the very act of affirming himself, man has lost himself. He has conquered the Earth, has created marvels, yet his assurance in himself has gone and he has lost his illusion and hope . . . . man is dwarfed and insignificant, he is left to contemplate the vast space he has discovered and the infinite emptiness in which there is no consolation, but only a godless terror.'

These words of Bardyeev aptly introduce my Epilogue on *The Healing Power*; which I am privileged and honoured to write as a 'conventional' medical doctor. However, I should indicate, I am a doctor who has experienced with sufficient proof to myself the existence of 'psychic phenomena' which are often rejected by the purist, scientific, material rationalists of our community.

As Bardyeev continues, 'When man broke away from the spiritual moorings of his life and tore himself from the deeps and went to the surface and became more superficial . . . when he lost the spiritual Centre of Being, he lost his own at the same time.'

I do not intend to cast any doubts on J Bernard Hutton's book; nor in any way to attempt to substantiate its contents. In no way have I had direct access to the evidence on investigation or case histories; but I do have personal knowledge of Mr Hutton as a man of painstaking thoroughness and honesty and one who is seeking the TRUTH in his work. I do, however, intend to offer supplementary relevant evidence, gleaned from many sources throughout the world, in the form of historical and scientific rationalistic 'facts' that are universally accepted by present-day scientists. I hope that this basis of relevant evidence in relation to *The Healing Power* will provoke any sceptics to consider and re-orientate their thinking and perhaps to persuade them other than to seek solace in their scepticism. I urge such people to cast aside what is perhaps a fear of the scientifically unknown in terms of facts and data which have not been proved under laboratory conditions. I urge such people to cast aside their almost automatic disregard of what they may consider to be 'out of the question'. I must stress that *this* is probably why most people, because of their rejection of what is apparently unrational, cannot and never will be able to come to terms with the concept of 'psychic phenomena'.

Especially today, as more techniques are rendering glimpses of the nature of such phenomena, I urge these sceptics to seek further knowledge founded on that important basis of a keen logical scientific training. Hence, I hope that Mr Hutton's book and my epilogue will result in the development of a rational approach to these glimpses and so result in scientific participation to the ultimate benefit of mankind. Perhaps, then, even though they will not accept 'proofs' of the cures of these diseases as demonstrated, they may care to accept a logical rationalisation as to the possibility of such cures. This acceptance will, I hope, be the first stage in the process of being convinced of the need to investigate further with clinically controlled tests.

One hundred and seventy years ago, Fichte wrote: 'Knowledge (ie scientific and linear logic) is not reality, just because it is knowledge .... it destroys and annihilates error (but it) cannot give us truth, for in itself it is absolutely empty.' May I thus ask the sceptic to think on the following question prior to rejecting spiritual healing? 'Is it that the knowledge, if indefinable, therefore must be unrealistic; or it is that in being undefinable – in twentieth century language – then it cannot be valid knowledge and hence has no value today?'

I somehow doubt that all our Einsteinian space-time basis of physics and matter is universally definable. Therefore, why cannot we accept other equally undefinable experiences and knowledge in our world, such as spiritual healing taking place in a human body mechanism of which our knowledge is far from complete and finite?

Therefore, I must bear in mind my position as a doctor registered with the General Medical Council and hence bound by its precepts which forbid any association with unregistered healers; thus, I, not wishing to indispose myself, intend to approach the concept from an *a priori* standpoint. In this way, I surely feel I cannot jeopardise myself or any other by rationalising logically the evidence gleaned from others towards my point of view. Thus, I sincerely hope I might bring this evidence as irrefutable in its own right, and thus determine *ipso facto* that spiritual healing can and does exist.

I recall a jingle intimating that objects cannot exist in the mind:

> *There once was a man who said 'God*
> *Must think it exceedingly odd*
> *If he finds that this tree*
> *Continues to be*
> *When there's no one about in the Quad.'*

His reply:

> *Dear Sir, Your astonishment's odd:*
> *I'm always about in the Quad.*
> *And that's why the tree*
> *Will continue to be,*
> *Since observed by Yours faithfully, God.*

Thus it is in the terms of provoking the reader, especially the doubtful-minded and perhaps conventional doctors and laymen who see spiritual healing as evil, or who deny its existence, or who fear the influence that I venture this critique. I do this in the humble yet burning hope that this occasion will be one where the criticism is creative and not self-seeking. You see, I feel in essence that criticism is always a form of intervention between the created work and its public. My criticism is not so much by quality of perception, but more by virtue of my analysis of the subject matter I wish to consider in relation to the present-day development of scientific knowledge of the structure and function of the human body and psyche. I seek to express this analysis for progressive and perceptive doctors and others who are inwardly and outwardly seeking benefit for their patients and suffering mankind.

I implore men of medicine to shun the velvet curtain of conventional conservatism and rigid dogmatism and seek that noble aim of the historical profession – that of furthering the art and science of healing.

In the same vein, I wish not overtly to prostitute that noble profession's public image, in perhaps potentiating and promoting a whimsical idealism of a 'panacea for all ills' in terms of spiritual healing. I do feel most strongly, however, that the time has come to study carefully orthodox medicine in relation to confirmed psychical research.

In this respect, it can be considered that Acupuncture, one ancient Chinese concept in healing, has done just this, and can be equated to this panacea state. Yet, subsequently, this concept has demanded scientific rationalism which has provoked detailed research with phenomenal results in terms of 'proof' of its truth and function. This truth and function as an expression of known body structure and methods of healing 'that work' is far from new; and that situation has resulted in the development of the science of body radiation field photographic technique.

The development of this technique has been necessary to convince the Acupuncture sceptics of the essence of the healing structure, ie, the human electromagnetic field forces, sometimes referred to as the 'aura'. The concept of the existence of an aura is not new as it was appreciated and utilised by the ancient Nai-Ching of China; the Kundalini Yoga; Buddhists, and Tibetans. Their concept of invisible human energy and radiations varying in relation to health, disease, human behaviour, and environmental change, has now become 'respectable' scientific knowledge. However, in the early days this concept was associated with religion and mysticism which, consequently, in the 'age of scientific enlightenment' became regarded 'as pagan superstitious nonsense. Similarly, I put it to you that one can consider spiritual healing to be a psychic manifestation of equivalent human energy and radiations; and that one can apply similarly rigid investigation to the end of determining yet another scientific development leading to 'respectable scientific knowledge'.

Surely, the spiritual healing of today is related to the 'laying on of hands' by the holy men of history.

I believe that the Acupuncture techniques now revitalised five thousand years later bridge a gap from the metaphysical and parabiological to the present-day medicine in so far that unidentified yet recordable body energies are common to both healing concepts.

This brings me to a medical precept that 'I treat, but Some One heals.'

I believe also that every healing is an Intelligent Act, involving the use of Forces about which we know little, whether that act is channelled through orthodox medicine or not. Thus, I feel that energy in healing, whether physical or mental (psychotherapy) must have an Ultimate Source in its action. This energy, which I will term psychic energy, is like all physical energy and equal to it in so far as it is devoid of an inherent value system. Thus it can be used as the consciousness of the person directing it desires. I doubt if any among us can deny the existence of physical energy. So, I cannot see how one can logically deny psychic energy. In this respect, it is interesting to observe that all the spiritual-healing masters have noted the essential applicat on of this psychic energy. So, although as yet the event of the healing process cannot be totally explained, the evidence of psychic and body energy is unavoidable as is equally the evidence of physical energy.

Let us consider now one or two concepts expressed by exponents of the use of this psychic energy.

Ronald Beasley in his book *Service of the Race* talks about the 'Soul of the Universe'. He believes that the great Universal Soul is the sum total of the Soul Essence (the physicists' electromagnetic force-centre) that exists in every atom. He maintains that if one can attune one's own soul essence to it, then an energy is transmitted that will heal and energise other earthly soul essences needing and balancing to produce replenishment and harmony. He believes that Christ acted in this way; and suggests that we should seek similar attunement. For this attunement he suggests a seeking of the rising of body vibrations by an enhancing of the inner self's spiritual awareness and consciousness of the oneness of our individual lives with the Universal Consciousness. Then the required Energy and Essence of Healing will flow out to the faithful recipient. I feel that this enhanced spiritual awareness means, as the evangelical Christians indicate, the situation of being awakened from within by the Holy Spirit and receiving Communication in order to relay Forces. This appears equivalent to the state of being 'born again into Christ' or reborn to God in terms of being moved by a force apart from one's own will. Thus this appears to be an experience of spiritual healing of the human spirit direct from the Source, and to be the situation of St Paul's rebirth which blinded him for three days.

I see an Ultimate Paradox, and hence may I say, a Spiritual Truth here, in so far that one must heal oneself in order to heal others and, conversely, that one heals oneself by healing others.

Edward Cayce sees this healing situation in terms of vibrations emanating from the Life Force and allowing the Healing Power to flow through to the sick person. In this way, I should like my reader to consider the Healing Ministry of Jesus Christ, Son of God.

It would be a bold critic who concluded that Christ's healing ministry and that ministry recorded of his subsequent apostles and converts to 'go forth and heal the sick' were unacceptable as fact because of the lack of proof demanded by the clinical medical scientists of today. To do this would negate all the evidence of the history, development, and power of the Christian Church and its influence throughout the ages until today. To do this would destroy the concept of Christ's very Being. Such a critical conclusion would not only be considered dangerously heretical but also would preclude the known Christian roots of the present-day medical profession. However, I find it difficult to conceive belief in part and not the whole; so why has the healing element, so deeply emphasised throughout Christian teaching, been dropped? New Testament evidence is clearly preferred in action, as also in instruction, to go forth believing that such healing can happen. As such healing did not involve drug and other therapies as part of the instruction, but only was to be based on belief and faith which together lead to the gift of healing.

Thus, one can logically conclude that the Power to Heal then in New Testament days was the same as today. And, obviously, *homo sapiens* is the same structurally and functionally today, and suffers the same disfigurements internally and externally and the same disfuntions. Thus, is THIS HEALING not the same POWER the spiritual healers of today have possessed within themselves in their high plain of spiritual awareness and which same POWER they are able to transfer as HEALING ENERGY?

Let us look now at some modern Russian evidence which might indicate the nature of the healing energy of the 'laying-on of hands'. I mean the Kirlian techniques of radiation photography, mentioned previously, which renders this healing energy 'visible'. Kirlian was working at the Kirov State University of Kacyakhotan in Alma Ata, with electronic microscopes. He showed them an 'energy body' surrounded and interpenetrated the physical body in relation to health, mood, tension, disease, thoughts, and fatigue, and that this energy changed alongside changes in the factors and in the environment. Kirlian and his school discovered the effects of these changes on what they termed the volatile energy body of bioplasmic today. I think this discovery equates accurately with the ancient concept of the human aura. I quote: 'Breathing changes the entire bioplasmic body and renews our reserves of vital energy and helps to equalise disturbed energy patterns' (ie diseased states physically, mentally, emotionally). I ask the reader to seek evidence in ancient Yoga techniques of health in this respect, and particularly in the breathing techniques where the belief is that breathing is a very significant kind of continuous communication with the Universal Life Energy. This means that Yoga believes that there is a constant interaction as the body harnesses these Vital Energies.

Gordon Turner feels that every living organism is constantly emanating patterns of energy which vary with age, health, disease, etc, and that these patterns are those expressed by psychics to be a reflexion of the physical, mental and spiritual state of that organism. He states that when the fine balance of these patterns is upset by undue emotion, disease or environmental factors, then the loss of energy outbalances its replacement. Is this replenishment not the role of the 'laying-on of hands' or spiritual healing?

In this form of psychic healing it is many times recorded that the patient feels a sensation of heat from the healer. The Kirlian apparatus in research was able to demonstrate a very difficult energy-pattern during the process of contact with the healer; and in fact shows the enery-intensity directing itself towards the diseased area (possibly because of the negative polarity of that area). Thus, it was concluded that psychic healing involves a transfer of energy from the bioplasmic body of the healer to that of the patient.

Also, it is known that Acupuncture points on the body can be 'seen' with the aid of this Kirlian photography technique and that the points demonstrated are identical with the ancient Chinese directives as to their locations. Furthermore, it has been recently demonstrated that Acupuncture therapy does not require needles to be inserted at these location points. In this respect results are being achieved by the use of directional electromagnetic forces which are concentrated on these location points. Similarly, the means and methods of focusing ultra-sonic and laser beams to the location points produce equivocal results to the needle techniques.

I believe, therefore, that there must be some link between the bioplasmic and the vital energy creation at location points in Acupuncture. I feel, therefore, that a similar link, using the directed contact of healing energy by the spiritual healer, must exist. This must exist especially in the case of the healer who has gained for himself an ability to absorb and transfer energy in a metaphysical sense by communication with his innerself and thence transferred this energy to his patient.

The Buddhists think in terms of the concept of *Karma*, of purposeful reincarnation, the continuity of life, the chance ability through freewill to determinate and thus balance the scales against their ego errors and hence against 'diseases'. Present-day investigations and scientific ideas reason that each body cell is essentially a galvanic battery which has the capacity to transform energy and thus that the whole body must be an electrical energy-system. This latter state as proven by Kirlian techniques substantiates the Buddhist and Yoga concepts; and indicates that diseases are represented as defects in the energy-system which are capable of being healed by Acupuncture and other techniques of energy contact therapy.

Thus, to return to Biblical concepts, I find that these are certainly not incompatible with the ideals of the 'concept of energy of living in man' and of the 'concept of no vital energy of living in dead man'. This Energy Force of Living, as distinct from dead, must be electrical or atomic in nature and so comparable with the vibratory or oscillatory state of physical energy. Thus on contact of the 'laying-on of hands' vibratory energy is felt as heat or light and as such is described, and hence is experienced as incorporating the spirit to mind and body.

Let me quote from the magazine *Scientific American* of February 1972, where some clinical trials on the physiology of meditation are described as having taken place at the University of California and Harvard medical units. Complex measurements were taken at regular intervals on cases practising transcendental meditation techniques. Oxygen, blood changes, heartbeat, skin energy resistance (electrical aura factors), brain waves and other changes were scientifically recorded and analysed during states of enhanced spiritual awareness and of experiencing 'cosmic' consciousness. During these states the ancient Chinese claimed that man is filled with a Vital Energy of Life Force which is part of the Total Life Force of the Universe. The Hindus call this state *Prana* (hence the drawing in of this Force in breathing exercises of Yoga-like meditation).

From this evidence and from my previous experience cannot spiritual healing be the absorption and transmission of this power and energy force as indicated in the physiology of meditation when there is self-attunement to the Source?

I know of no greater Christian truism than that each of us is Part

Of God ('created in his Own image' means this, I am sure), who is that Universal Power and Energy. In this respect, therefore, and incorporating the recorded Biblical evidence, I would venture to say that to *deny* the possibility of spiritual healing is to deny the existence of Creation and the possession of the Supreme Energy which is within ourselves.

I think also of the great Christian mystics – did they not through relaxation, prayer, and meditation attune themselves to the Power we have now seen demonstrated electromagnetically and physiologically?

Let us approach the picture of spiritual healing from another standpoint. The World Health Organisation defines health as a 'state of physical, mental and social wellbeing and not merely the absence of disease or debility'. Therefore, in time of life-processes, the concept is that man is a balanced creation, ie health can be understood only within a concept of dynamic equilibrium of the body's internal and external environments. Or – if we think in terms of another format of definition – health is harmony, disease is discord. This means that the living organism is in a state of continuous balance of its physical, mental, and spiritual attributes in relation to the environment. Hermes, the Thrice Great, stated: 'Everything flows out and in, everything has its tides, all things rise and fall, rhythm compensates.'

Thus, all attempts at healing in situations of discord and disharmony, which we call physical, mental or emotional diseases, are in reality attempts to regulate and restore the normal rhythms or equilibrium, irrespective of the media by which the attempt is made. Thus, the defect must be known in terms of this body rhythm which I see as an electrical body balance of energy forces, positive, negative and neutral. These forces are the sum total of all the electrical entities that make up the body, ie the cells. Thus the energy flows and maintains the dynamic equilibrium of the body in relation to the internal and external environments.

Our scientific methods have proved that electromagnetic waves pass over the body and away from it (the aura of the ancients again). These waves exist in terms of positive, negative and neutral. Their existence is equivalent to the Yin, Yang of Yoga, and Acupunture concepts and, as mentioned previously, they have a direct relationship to health maintainance and healing situations. This is seen as the characteristic Life Force of the living as distinct from the dead.

I suggest now that one considers the appreciation that all matter, whether living or dead, is made up of atoms consisting of protons, neutrons, and electrons each with its own force-centre and in constant motion and vibration. Thus, I maintain that the Life Force of living beings must be something more than the electrical fields of the composite atoms. Furthermore, we know that all the human organism is controlled by innumerable nerve impulses of electrical flow and electrochemical ionic exchanges which are set in motion from conception. So, the positive, negative and neutral concept must have validity especially as we can now scientifically demonstrate it internally and externally in the body. Thus, disease can be expressed rationally in terms of defects of these electrical and electrochemical functions which has become unbalanced and inconstant.

Healing must therefore be concerned with the *imbalance* and must be concerned with the *restoration* of the *positive (Yang)* and the *negative (Yin) forces.*

These forces, therefore, express the state of health, mentally and physically and the state of well-being socially and environmentally. The radiations of these field forces of the states as indicated by the human aura are therefore expressed in terms of disturbances in the vibratory concept in relation to the existence of disease in any of the physical, mental, spiritual or adjustment to internal or external environmental spheres.

Thus, health is the state of balanced vibrations and perfect harmony of the full and complete radiating vital energy in the physical and psychic bodies, as with every atom of the whole body and for that matter of the total universe.

So, could it not be again that the spiritual healer plays his part by restoring the ultimate vibrations to polarity perfection and so overcoming the interferences of balanced energy flow by disease? Thus by so doing the spiritual healer restores the body structure and function to health and harmony.

Therefore, from my whole reasoning from religious and historical concepts, and practical evidence; from the scientific discovery of life forces and relative phenomena; I see clearly and rationally a validity for the concept and existence of spiritual healing.

I feel *now* is the time to attempt to assess the evidence in J Bernard Hutton's book in relation to that of these other sources and to strike a balanced reasoning on that evidence in relation to scientific knowledge today. I suggest this evidence should be seen in perspective to the rigid dogmatisms of anti-projection that are purported by the medical profession's *alma mater.*

I believe that orthodox science and conventional medicine can no longer ignore the facts concerning psychic healing and curing incurables.

I implore that scientific minds should explore all their thinking and seek to rise above the threshold and leave no area irrevocably closed to conscious inspection and investigation.

I believe that the concept of spiritual healing in relation to the science of body balance and the proven ability of mankind to allow himself to become the channel for God's Healing Energy must be developed; so bringing the fullest orthodox scientific, medical powers together with the psychic forces to the benefit of the many in need.

I feel the recognition of psychic healing will come as Acupuncture has come.

In some respects, the Western World in relation to spiritual healing, has not only lost the way – it has lost the map!

The appeal I make to the reader of this epilogue is he should shed the ego and realise with St Bonaventura that God is an Intelligible Sphere whose centre is everywhere and whose circumference nowhere.'

Thus I conclude that every healing is an intelligible act involving the use of forces we are only just coming to understand.

Finally, I heartily recommend Mr Hutton's work for all who have any interest in healing, and end with the aphorism:

> *We move from the simple to the complex:*
> *The obvious is the last thing we learn.*

I am indebted to the following in writing the Epilogue:
Mr William P Lawrence for his presence, help, and sincere understanding; Sally Hammond for her book *We Are All Healers;* Edgar Cayce for his 281 Series 'Spiritual Communications'; Dr Charlotte Bach, Ph D for her *Studies in Human Ethology* and her concept of the Pythagorean World Soul; R K Wallace and Herbert Benson for *Physiology of Meditation;* and to Mr J Bernard Hutton for stimulating me to 'think on these lines'.

APPENDIX

WHEN I CONSULTED Leah Doctors' records I expected
I would find a neat card-index indicating all the patients
who had received direct contact healing and absent healing. These cards
would have shown the date treatment commenced, the progressive
stages of the patient's recovery (or failure), neat entries recording the
number of healing treatments received, and the final results from the
treatments. From these cards I intended to compose charts and statistics
showing types of illnesses, the numbers of patients completely cured,
the numbers of those who had shown *some* improvement only, and the
numbers of those whom spiritual healing hasn't helped at all.

But Leah Doctors, without adequate staff, has no business filing
system. When I asked her to see her records of patients, she gave me
a slightly amused, quizzical glance and led me to a bureau. Its drawers
were crammed with letters stuffed in higgledy-piggledy. They were all
letters from patients, Leah told me. If they would help me with my
book, I could see them and use them.

After examining these letters, and realising there was no neat
card-index record of Leah's patients, it was obvious I hadn't the material
to compose a fully documented, case-history record of Dr Chang's and
Leah's healings. Periodically Leah had a clean-out when stacks of letters
were simply dumped. So it is impossible to estimate how many records
of cures, small improvements or failures have been lost in this way.

In many cases I could find only one letter from a patient from which
it was obvious that others had been written during a long course of
absent healing. Later, when I communicated with the most interesting
letter-writers, many replied asking me not to mention their names or
illnesses in my book. Others adopted a more menacing attitude and
forbade me to use in any circumstances information contained in a
letter. Other patients had moved and their new addresses were unknown. A disappointing large number of people simply ignored my
letters.

Leah Doctors was not surprised at this frustrating lack of response.
She has grown quite philosophical about indifference.

'When people are sick and need me, they are grateful,' she said. 'But when they are fit and well, they soon forget they once needed help. That's good. People should be thankful, but shouldn't keep remembering back to suffering. The important thing is that they've been healed. That's all that matters.'

Some of the following case-histories which Leah Doctors permitted me to publish, will seem incomplete. I have condensed my reports of these cures because this book is not an encyclopaedia. It would have been pointless to include all the case-histories of Dr Chang's and Leah Doctors' many hundreds of patients even if I'd been able; dull and repetitious as well.

But the following case-histories may serve sceptics to have a second look at spiritual healing, instead of dismissing it without trial. They may also give solace to those sick and medically incurable people who have never thought of trying whether spiritual healing could help them.

CASE-HISTORIES

CONTACT HEALING

Mr Richard Harvey

A diabetic for many years. Forty-eight units of insulin prescribed. Informed his illness is incurable and can only be kept in check by drugs. A victim of side effects of insulin; loss of energy, tiredness, and apathy.

Mr Harvey consulted Leah after being recommended by another diabetic who had been cured by Dr Chang. His first treatment was in March 1954. After the first treatment his insulin dosage was reduced by six units. He attended healing sessions twice a week for six months. At the end of that period he was cured.

The doctors and nurses at the hospital were not surprised when they declared him free of diabetes and discharged him. By this time they had records of several diabetic patients who had inexplicably lost their diabetes symptoms after treatment by Dr Chang.

Mr Angus MacMillan

Fifty-seven years of age. Chronic asthma. Bedridden at home for nine years. Continuously losing weight. A case for serious medical concern.

In 1955, Mr MacMillan was assisted to make the short journey from his home to Leah Doctors' healing sanctuary. He underwent weekly healing sessions with Dr Chang for ten weeks. Even after the first treatment he felt very much better. The following morning he had the strength to get up alone. After a month he went for lengthy walks. At the end of the healing sessions his health was completely restored.

Mrs Anne Lewis

In August 1955, Leah received a telephone plea from Mrs Lewis. She was distraught. Her son, Johnny, who was five years of age, was suffering from leukaemia. The hospital doctors gave him six months to live. Could Leah do anything?

'I took a bus straight away,' Leah told me. 'Johnny's mother opened the door, showed me into her sitting-room and then went for Johnny. She carried him downstairs in her arms. Although he was five, he looked the size of a child of two; very thin and withered. I asked Mrs Lewis to leave the room and I gave Johnny spiritual healing while he sat on my lap. I gave him a sweet, made friends with him, and soothed him until he relaxed in my arms.

'Then Dr Chang came to me and moved my right hand in gentle

stroking movements over his back, arms, and legs. After twenty minutes or so I told Johnny: "Stand up." He said he couldn't. But I insisted. I told him he'd received healing that had made him better. He believed me and tried. He *could* stand. Then I got him standing first on one leg, and then on the other, half a dozen times. Then I told him to run around the table. He didn't want to. He said he couldn't. But I assured him he could and, when he did, the colour came back into his cheeks, his eyes grew bright, and he began to laugh with happiness as he ran.

'Mrs Lewis came into the room, unable to believe her ears when she heard him laugh. When she saw him running around she began to weep. I explained that Johnny was benefiting from the healing rays, told her she must encourage Johnny to keep exercising, and said I'd call back two days later. When I did, Mrs Lewis was elated. The doctor had called meanwhile and had said Johnny was fit enough to go to school.

'When Johnny went to the Children's Hospital for his regular check-up, blood tests showed he had no trace of leukaemia. After other tests, the specialist told Mrs Lewis that Johnny need not be brought to the hospital again until a routine check was made in a year's time.'

Hospital routine tests in 1956 and 1957 confirmed that Johnny had no symptoms of leukaemia.

In 1972, Johnny Lewis now works as a motor mechanic in a garage and at the age of twenty-two is fit and well.

Mr Alfred Bishop

A victim of severe shock. Left arm continually trembling, deafness in the left ear, headaches and dizziness.

Mr Bishop was under the care of a hospital. Specialists had told him there *was* hope of a cure, but it would take a very long time. He had received hospital attention for months and had to take drugs which made no perceptible difference to his condition.

After one healing session with Dr Chang, Mr Bishop went home feeling very tired, went to bed, and slept for forty-eight hours. When he awoke he was completely cured.

When I investigated his case in 1972, there had been no return of any of his severe shock symptoms. He could hear in his left ear.

Mrs Mary Hibbert

Attending hospital for anaemia. High blood resin. Stomach distended. Forward curvature. Weakness and listlessness. After many months of hospital treatment, Mrs Hibbert's condition did not improve. The hospital doctors admitted she was making no progress.

Mrs Hibbert received healing rays treatment from Dr Chang from April to July 1956. After three treatments she had gained eighteen pounds, her blood pressure was reduced, her weight was normal, and her appetite improved. At the end of the healing rays treatment she felt she was back to normal health. The hospital doctors agreed. They discharged her.

Miss Daphne Gingall

A registered diabetic for twenty-one years. Under constant hospital treatment. Insulin: seventy-eight units.

Miss Gingall was thirty-three when she consulted Dr Chang in 1958. She was told by Dr Chang that her illness was deep-rooted and would require many weekly healing rays treatments. After the first healing session, her insulin intake was reduced by the hospital doctor by six units. Every month thereafter her insulin intake was reduced. By 1961 it was down to thirty-two units. While receiving hospital treatment prior to her first visit to Leah Doctors' Healing Sanctuary, her insulin intake had slowly increased. Under Dr Chang is steadily decreased.

Miss Gingall left England in 1961 and was compelled to abandon contact healing treatment with Dr Chang. I have been unable to discover her whereabouts to investigate her present state of health.

'Carry on the good work'

Dr Chang had eight diabetic patients who were out-patients at the same London hospital. All eight were steadily decreasing their insulin intake and the chief physician at the hospital had taken a great interest in the results that Dr Chang was obtaining. Among *all* the physician's diabetic patients, Dr Chang's eight patients were the *only* ones steadily decreasing insulin intake.

Mr Jack Doctors thought this might be the precise moment to try to help all this physician's diabetic patients. So, on Jack's prompting, Leah suggested to the chief physician that he should send her six additional adult and six child diabetics so that Dr Chang could heal them under test conditions.

The chief physician was personally extremely interested in the suggestion. But he was bound by General Medical Council regulations. These forbade him to co-operate with Leah Doctors – an unregistered practitioner. In a personal letter he regretted he was obliged to decline her suggestion. But he hoped she would 'carry on the good work' with all those diabetic patients who personally approached her and asked for treatment.

Mrs Rita Messin

Diabetic. Attending hospital for ten years. Insulin intake: fifty units.

Healing rays treatment began in March 1961. After two-weekly healing sessions for two months, insulin intake reduced to ten units. After four months' healing rays application by Dr Chang, the hospital doctor declared the patient cured of diabetis.

Gerald Baxter

Diabetic. Thirteen years of age. Receiving hospital treatment for four years, since he was nine years old. Insulin intake: sixty-eight units.

Gerald's healing rays treatment commenced on 12th May 1962. On 26th May his insulin intake was reduced to sixty-two units. On 2nd June reduced to fifty-eight units. On 16th July, reduced to thirty-two units. In September 1962, Gerald was declared cured of diabetes.

Alan Waters

Diabetic. Fourteen years of age. Under hospital care for seven years – half his life. Insulin intake: eighty units.

Alan visited Leah's Healing Sanctuary in 1962. Dr Chang's healing rays sessions were successful. Alan's intake of insulin was reduced swiftly. His recovery from diabetes was considered extraordinary.

Mrs Eve Gardener

Diabetic. Under hospital care. Regular insulin intake: sixty units.

After Mrs Gardner's first healing rays treatment in September 1962, she declared she felt much better. After five treatments she was discharged from hospital. She was free of diabetes.

Mrs Mabel Tisch

Diabetic. Under hospital care. Insulin intake: ten units.

Attended healing rays sessions with Dr Chang until insulin intake was reduced to four units. She then ceased healing treatment.

Mrs Louisa Leston

Diabetic. Under hospital care. Regular insulin intake: forty-two units.

Mrs Leston began healing rays treatment with Dr Chang in 1963. Insulin intake steadily reduced until she was declared cured of diabetes.

Mrs Ivy Wakefield

Diabetic. Eleven-and-a-half years a hospital out-patient.

Mrs Wakefield received Dr Chang's healing rays treatment from the autumn of 1968 until November 1968. She then wrote the following letter to Leah Doctors on 4th November 1968:

Dear Mrs Doctors,

      I hardly know how to begin this special letter to you

because I feel quite overcome by the wonderful verdict given me at Brighton Hospital. When I tell you I've been a regular visitor there for 11½ years, at regular intervals of three or six months, you will understand how I felt when given a *complete discharge*. I sat rooted to the chair, scarcely hearing the doctor giving me advice, and telling me not to think I'm really cured – but with care and a tablet a day, I am not to visit them again, unless anything unforseen happened, etc. He is writing to my doctor to tell him.

I came out of the hospital and sat down on a seat on the deserted seafront and burst into tears, with gratitude and relief. Even now I can't believe it; I feel so happy.

All thanks to you and Dr Chang. It's truly a miracle and I wish I had known about you long ago. . . .

Miss Jean Bell

Miss Bell was twenty-one years of age when she consulted Dr Chang. She had been deaf in her left ear since birth; and partially deaf in her right ear. A hospital specialist said she could be given no medical assistance, apart from a hearing-aid.

Dr Chang predicted a lengthy healing treatment and Miss Bell attended six months before her hearing was completely restored. Her doctor described her cure as 'some sort of miracle'.

Mr Clarke

Mr Clarke received a blow on the head at the age of five which caused deafness in his left ear. He later became partly deaf in the right ear. Some consultants thought this might have some connection with the deafness in his left ear. Mr Clarke spent about £300 on special medical treatment, including deep-ray treatment. He was reluctant to accept the hospital consultant's verdict that nothing could be done to save what little hearing he still possessed.

At Mr Clarke's first healing session, Dr Chang told him that he could cure his right ear, but doubted he could do anything for the left ear. Full hearing was eventually restored to Mr Clarke's right ear.

While receiving this treatment, Mr Clarke began to pass blood in his urine. His doctor recommended him to hospital. But Dr Chang treated this symptom with healing rays and the trouble disappeared after three visits.

Mrs Lily Ferguson

Mrs Ferguson was resident in Africa where she had been attending hospital. After being X-rayed and submitting to other tests, she had been informed she suffered from a chronic cancer of the stomach. She was warned by hospital specialists she had a life expectation of about six months.

Mrs Ferguson hoped Britain's National Health Service might be able to help her. She came to London and attended the Hackney Hospital. Her X-ray and other tests confirmed what the African specialists had told her. Her time was running out fast.

Mrs Ferguson visited Dr Chang in September 1962, and received healing rays treatment for about thirty minutes. Dr Chang said he would be able to cure her if she returned for more treatment the following day.

After her first healing rays treatment, Mrs Ferguson felt tired; she had a rectal discharge and slept very heavily that night. The following day, Dr Chang performed a spirit operation. During the following few days the cancer would disappear through her bowels, he told her.

Ten years later, in 1972, Mrs Ferguson recalled: 'Two days after I was given the second treatment the cancer came out through my bowels without any pain, exactly as Dr Chang told me it would. Ever since I have been in perfect health. Everybody tells me I look twenty years younger.'

Mrs Martha Levine

This unfortunate lady had suffered arthritis for forty years and needed pain-relieving drugs to subdue the continual pain she endured. Her disease affected her spinal column, displaced her shoulder blade, and was especially virulent in her left knee.

Her first healing session with Dr Chang was in November 1962. He told her he could relieve her suffering, but could *not* cure her disease. If she persisted with prolonged healing rays treatment she would eventually be able to move around more freely, and without pain. After the treatment, an arthritic lump in Mrs Levine's right armpit disappeared. During the following weeks of healing her pain decreased steadily until, by June 1963, she no longer required pain-relieving drugs. She was able to go out for walks and shop with ease.

The healing rays treatment was then discontinued. Dr Chang could do no more for her. As he had predicted, she was free from pain, and could get around. After forty years of continuous pain and immobility, these blessings made Mrs Levine feel she had been given new life.

Mrs Margaret Marshall

As a consequence of infantile paralysis, Mrs Marshall had suffered osteo-arthritis for fifteen years. Her right hip was so diseased that the lower part of 'her back had fused into it. She could walk only with the greatest of difficulty. She needed help to descend stairs or cross the road. At night she could not sleep without the aid of drugs. For years she had undergone physiotherapy which gave her only very slight relief.

'After two spiritual healings with Mrs Doctors, my nerves are steady and my hips are very much better,' said Mrs Marshall. 'I can sleep without pain and my walking has improved greatly. My back is more flexible.'

Dr Chang had warned Mrs Marshall in advance that he could *not* cure her. But at the end of a series of healing rays treatments, like Mrs Levine, she was freed from pain and could move around more easily.

Mrs Caroline Ledger

Mrs Ledger had an abdominal hernia and was scheduled to undergo a surgical operation. After four spirit operations performed by Dr Chang, she was informed by the hospital doctor that her hernia had disappeared. Her surgical operation was cancelled.

Mrs Helen Warr

Mrs Warr had worn a surgical belt for fifteen years. As a result of a surgical operation she had a weak spine. This contributed to a serious stomach condition.

In 1962 she had two healing treatments from Dr Chang. Afterwards she was able to dispense with her surgical belt and was relieved of her stomach cramps.

Mrs Joan Bugens

Mrs Bugens had large, painful, unsightly varicose veins. She wore thick elastic stockings, and long dresses to conceal the stockings. She was given healing treatment by Dr Chang in 1962.

'I was able to give away my elastic stockings and wear short dresses,' she said afterwards. 'A new life opened up for me when I got rid of those awful veins!'

Mr Ernest Edwards

Disseminated sclerosis, a progressive disease of the nervous system. Small areas of the spinal cord and the brain are attacked and cease to function. No effective treatment is known to modern medicine. Mr Edwards had been told by hospital doctors that nothing could be done for him and he was discharged into the care of his local doctor. He suffered frequent bouts of pain, was unable to walk, and could stand up only with an effort; and then only for a few minutes at a time.

When Mr Edwards attended Leah Doctors' healing sanctuary in August 1963, he was carried into the healing-room. After a number of healing rays sessions Mr Edwards was still not completely cured. But he was free of pain, was able to walk, and can live a near-normal life.

Mrs Maria Kolita

Mrs Kolita was scheduled to udergo a surgical operation for a fibroid growth. She had a second medical problem. For ten years her marriage had been childless. She and her husband longed to have a baby.

In 1963, Dr Chang performed a spirit operation on Mrs Kolita which removed her fibroid. He also focused healing rays upon her womb.

Mrs Kolita became pregnant before she was discharged by the hospital, where medical tests established that her fibroid growth had disappeared. She later gave birth to a healthy baby.

Miss Florence Rich

Miss Rich suffered ill health and nagging pain from haemorrhoids. Surgery was recommended by the hospital consultant as the only means to restore her good health.

After one healing session with Dr Chang, when he performed a spirit operation, Miss Rich's piles withered away. Within a month she felt fit and well. The surgical operation was cancelled.

Mrs Granfield

Mrs Granfield was scheduled to undergo a surgical operation for a stomach ulcer. She visited Leah Doctors' healing santuary in 1964 – while waiting to hear from the hospital when to report for the proposed surgery. After five healing sessions, she was healed by Dr Chang. When she eventually heard from the hospital and appeared there, she was discharged after thorough medical examinations. The scheduled surgical operation was cancelled.

Mr Harold Sillett

Mr Sillett had suffered from colitis for two years. This inflammation of the colon depresses the general health and causes severe discomfort and diarrhoea. Despite the medical attention he was given throughout this period, the disease did not diminish.

After two healing treatments in 1964, Dr Chang cured Mr Sillett.

Mr William A Davis

Mr Davis consulted Dr Chang about a dull, nagging pain in his abdomen. Dr Chang diagnosed a grumbling appendix. He performed a spirit operation in March 1965. Following the spirit operation, Mr Davis experienced soreness which disappeared after a few days. Since then, he has had no repetition of the pain.

Mrs Rita Moore

Mrs Moore was booked to enter hospital for a surgical operation to remove a growth in 1966, when she visited Dr Chang. She underwent a spirit operation. When subsequently re-examined at the hospital, all traces of her growth had disappeared. The operation was cancelled.

Mrs Kathleen Long

In 1964, Mrs Long suffered a stroke. For the following two years she endured considerable discomfort, stomach pains, and nervous dyspepsia. In the autumn of 1966, Mrs Long had six healing sessions with Dr Chang.

'It was wonderful to be free from the continual pain,' she stated afterwards. 'For two years I had been having treatment from my doctor; yet after only six visits to Mrs Doctors, life took on a new outlook. I regained all the confidence I'd lost after having my stroke.'

Mr B Turner

A hospital consultant told Mr Turner that he did not believe the medical treatment being used on him would meet with success. He said Mr Turner had stomach ulcers and a surgical operation would be necessary.

Mr Turner visited Leah Doctors' Healing Sanctuary in April 1968. Dr Chang said he would perform a spirit operation which would dispose of the ulcers. But there might be a residue of little lumps which would require an additional spirit operation later. Mr Turner underwent the spirit operation and described what transpired when he returned to hospital for a check-up:

'I had a long session with the surgeon. He was mystified. After a long and thorough examination he said that all he could find wrong with me were some little lumps. He admitted he was puzzled and asked me to return to the hospital later. He wanted to keep me under observation.'

The surgeon was even more mystified the next time Mr Turner visited him. In the meantime Dr Chang had performed the second spirit operation which he'd forecast would remove the little lumps. The surgeon searched a long time to find the little lumps and eventually, much perplexed, confessed he could find no trace of them.

Mrs Muriel Johnstone

Mrs Johnstone had suffered a hearing defect since youth. She had visited many ear specialists in Brighton and London. The best that could be done for her was to supply her with a hearing-aid. It helped very little. For all practical purposes, she was completely deaf.

Mrs Johnstone was eighty-seven years of age when she visited Leah Doctors' Healing Sanctuary in April 1969. Leah placed her hands upon Mrs Johnstone's ears and she sensed a slight burning inside her head. After three healing sessions Mrs Johnstone was able to hear perfectly.

Mr Cyril Fugeman

Mr Fugeman was a gardener. He was often off work because manual labour aggrevated his physical condition. He suffered severe colitis. This caused general depression, stomach pains, diarrhoea, and loss of weight. He was under medical treatment but did not respond to it.

When Mr Fugeman visited Dr Chang in July 1969, he had lost so much weight that he was down to eight stone. After weekly healing rays treatment for two months Mr Fugeman recovered from his illness and gained two and a half stone in weight.

Nurse J Fenton

Nurse Fenton had a cyst on her right breast. The hospital surgeon recommended immediate surgery.

Dr Chang performed a spirit operation in 1970 – just before Nurse Fenton was due for her surgical operation. The hospital surgeon could subsequently find no trace of the cyst.

Mrs K Jenkins

Mrs Jenkins was losing her hair. It came away in handfuls. She was horror-stricken at the thought of impending baldness.

Mrs Jenkins consulted Dr Chang in July 1971. From the first healing session onwards, her hair ceased to fall out. During the following weeks it gained strength and regrew.

Mrs Dorothy Neal

Glaucoma is an eye condition when the pressure of the fluid within the eyeball becomes excessive. Mrs Neal had suffered glaucoma for seven years. Her vision was blurred and she had the greatest difficulty in reading. She received continual treatment but her vision did not improve.

Hoping that spiritual healing might do more for her than medical care could, Mrs Neal visited Leah Doctors' healing sanctuary. She began healing rays treatment from Dr Chang in December 1971. Her treatment is continuing as this book goes to press.

'Now I can see to read better,' Mrs Neal told me in Autumn 1972. 'The blurring goes away quickly after I relax, and it does not return as quickly as it used to. My eyes are much clearer and brighter in appearance.'

Dr Chang assured me he would improve Mrs Neal's eyes; but she needs long and persistant healing rays treatment, he declared.

After two-and-a-half years of healing rays treatment, the consultant opthalmologist said (in February 1974) that her eye-tests show great improvement in her vision. Mrs Neal has faith in Dr Chang and visits for contact healing twice a week 'to speed things up'.

Mrs Betty Brown

Is there a cure for lung cancer? Mrs Brown is certain there is – through spiritual healing.

In October 1971, the hospital doctor diagnosed that Mrs Brown had cancer in her left lung. A surgical operation was recommended.

When consulted, Dr Chang told Mrs Brown she had a deep-seated cancer with large and extensive growths. He performed a spirit operation and combined this with focusing his healing rays on to the cancer so as to break up the growths. He told Mrs Brown that as a result of his concentrated healing rays treatment the cancerous growths would discharge from her body through her bowels. He warned her that she must not be startled by its appearance, which would be black and evil-smelling.

Two weeks later, Mrs Brown called to give thanks. She no longer had pain in her lung, she could breathe freely and she could lie on her side at night, which she hadn't been able to do for the past three years.

After another examination at the hospital, medical consultants confirmed that she was free of any lung cancer. No surgical operation was necessary.

Mrs Mary Beecham

In the spring of 1972, Mrs Beecham attended Leah Doctors' Healing Sanctuary. She complained of a complete prolapse of her bowels. She had suffered stomach upsets since her teens and had been under constant medical supervision. For more than twenty years she had been on a strict diet. A recent severe bout of diarrhoea had left her so weak she felt she had not much longer to live.

She noticed an improvement in her condition as soon as she began healing rays treatment with Dr Chang. Although her condition required more treatment, she told me: 'Though I'm not yet cured, I am a new woman. I'm full of energy now. In fact, I am painting and decorating the house as well as doing the gardening. That's apart from shopping, my housework and other chores. My face has filled out and everyone says how much better and brighter I look.'

Mrs Beecham continued receiving treatment from Dr Chang, and in February 1974 it was confirmed that she was cured.

Miss Wynn Clark

Miss Clark described her experience at Leah Doctors' Healing Sanctuary as follows:

'For eighteen years I have tried various means to get rid of a lump on the paratoid gland under my left ear. An operation was suggested by my doctor, with the warning that it could cause the loss of my voice and partial paralysis on one side of my face. Who wants that! I am an actress. I couldn't afford to take the risk.'

This lump was a great handicap to Miss Clark in her profession. It was unsightly, and to disguise it she wore a long wig. Casting directors selected her only for roles of elderly women who could wear a large, enveloping wig.

Miss Clark disclosed that six years earlier she'd tried spiritual healing.

'This stopped the lump enlarging but as it did not go away, my healer agreed I should seek other spiritual healing help. For the past seven months I've been attending Mrs Doctors' Healing Sanctuary every week. Although my complaint is not yet completely cleared up, slowly but surely Dr Chang is changing the nature of the lump. It's now broken up into separate pieces and doesn't swell out from my face as it did before. After each visit it becomes softer and smaller. It's stopped causing me discomfort. I can carry on with my work and I can sleep on my left side without being aware of the lump. Apart from all this, I feel I'm being helped in my general health. If I hurry down to Hove feeling fatigued and overworked, I always know I'll be leaving the Healing Sanctuary rested and restored in spirit.'

As this book goes to press, Miss Clark is attending Leah Doctors' Healing Sanctuary for treatment and making satisfactory progress.

Mrs Eileen Dawes

Mrs Dawes had a severely strained leg muscle. It caused a great deal of pain. Her doctor informed her it would be many weeks before her leg was better; meanwhile she must be prepared to bear the pain.

After one treatment with Dr Chang, Mrs Dawes reported: 'I've no more pain at all and my leg is perfectly all right now.'

Mrs A Morley

Haemorrhoids can be extremely painful. Mrs Morley's condition was so serious she could not sit down without agony. She was sixty-three years of age. Her doctors advised her to undergo surgery.

Mrs Morley made the long journey from Preston to Hove. She was surprised when Dr Chang told her she would need four successive days of healing rays treatment. She had planned to return home the following day. But she complied with Dr Chang's requirements.

'Dr Chang took over from Mrs Doctors, made me lie on my side and plucked at my clothes, as though plucking something away,' Mrs Morley stated. 'On the fourth day I was annoyed because I wasn't feeling any better. I wondered how I could sit six hours on the bus, all the way from London to Preston. Dr Chang said I mustn't lose faith. But it was me suffering the pain and I thought it was all baloney.

'Then Dr Chang said I had a fibroid in my stomach. It was true my stomach did swell up at times. But I didn't bother about it much because it didn't give me real discomfort, so I hadn't mentioned it. Dr Chang plucked at this too. But none of it seemed to do any good.

'So I went away feeling it had all been a waste of time and money. But the very next day I began to get better. As God is my judge, I've never been troubled since, either by my piles or my fibroids. All this was in 1964 and my family and my doctor can vouch for it. Now it's 1972, and at the age of seventy-two I've no trouble at all with my health. I'm not a deluded old fool; I thank Dr Chang in my prayers.'

Mrs Betty Raine

In April 1972, Mrs Raine suffered from an unpleasant throat condition that was extremely painful and made talking very difficult. Mrs Raine visited Leah Doctors' Healing Sanctuary in November 1972, and reported: 'She placed her hands on my throat and gave me spiritual healing. Since then my throat problem has cleared up and now gives me no trouble whatever.'

Mr Jeremy Smith

Mr Smith attended hospital and it was diagnosed that he had a tumour behind his left eye. He was given radium treatment; it was hoped this would improve his condition. Unfortunately, his eye trouble became worse. He had constant irritant pain – 'as though I had pepper in my eyes,' he said. Following the radium treatment he suffered eye haemorrhage. He now had to put drops in his eyes because the tear ducts had ceased to function. While receiving medical treatment his vision deteriorated until he was blind in the left eye, and almost blind in the right eye. The hospital consultant told him there was nothing more they could do to help restore his vision.

Mr Smith consulted Leah Doctors in October 1972. After five healing rays treatments, the peppery, burning pain in his eyes ceased and he needed to put drops in his eyes only once a day. At the beginning of November he had an eye-test at the hospital. He could read four lines on the eye-testing board with his right eye. Previous to Dr Chang's healing rays treatment it had been impossible for him to read at all with this eye. The left eye was the eye affected by a tumour. Previously he had been quite blind in this eye. Now, tests showed he could distinguish light from dark shadows.

In December 1972, Dr Chang assured me that he could restore Mr Smith's sight with continuous healing rays treatment. He declared that the tumour was disintegrating.

Mr Smith continued receiving treatment from Dr Chang, and in October 1973 was provided with glasses by his opthalmic surgeon which enabled him to resume his desk job. He had been out of work for three years, but Dr Chang's healing rays treatment helped him return to a normal way of life.

Mr Angus James

When Mr James visited Leah Doctors' healing sanctuary in August 1972, his leg was extremely swollen and painful. Hospital consultants had informed him that his leg was cancerous, the cancer was spreading, and amputation of his leg was essential.

Mr James received fourteen daily healing rays treatments from Dr Chang. At the end of the healing sessions, the cancerous lump in his leg had disappeared and so had all the swelling. Mr James was free of pain and felt in excellent health.

He had an appointment to be examined by a London specialist; the consultation had been arranged before Mr James commenced healing rays treatment from Dr Chang. But he felt so well he didn't attend hospital for the consultation. In March 1974 he declared he was completely healed. 'He's running his newsagent business,' Leah informed me in the spring of 1974. 'I see him at times in his shop. He is quite well – no pain in his leg at all. . . .'

Mrs M Martin

Mrs Martin visited Leah in October 1963. She suffered from stomach pains and haemorrhoids. After prolonged medical treatment she could not find relief and a surgical operation was proposed. After her first healing treatment, Mrs Martin wrote:

Dear Mrs Doctors,

I promised to write to let you know how I have been this week since I visited you last Saturday. I am very thankful to say I have been free from pain in my tummy since my visit. This is quite something after all the years of pain I've suffered. I am much better, although I still feel I have an obstruction which stops the proper action of my bowels. . . .

Mrs Martin had one more healing session with Dr Chang after which she was declared cured of her complaint.

Mrs S Tidy

Mrs Tidy had internal pain, haemorrhoids, and a nervous condition. She lost a great deal of weight. She was under the hospital for a long time and when a surgical operation was proposed in August 1970, she wrote to Leah Doctors for an appointment.

Unfortunately, Leah was heavily committed and could not make an appointment until 21st September. But she wrote to Mrs Tidy that she would be giving her absent healing meanwhile.

On 20th August 1970, Mrs Tidy wrote the following letter to Leah:

Dear Mrs Doctors,

Although I still have the wretched piles, my general health is improving enormously. My appetite is much better and I have put on quite a lot of weight. I have tried to do this for six years without any success until now. I had great hollows in my cheeks and looked awful. Now my face is changing, the hollows are gone and I'm plumper in the body. I feel this is the beginning of a complete recovery. All sorts of people have told me how well I look – nobody has said this for years – I feel so comforted to know you are doing so much for me. I can't tell you what a relief it is to know you are bringing me alive again.

After her spiritual healing appointment on 21st September, at which she underwent a spirit operation, she felt considerable improvement. Shortly after the spirit operation, her haemorrhoids disappeared and her general health was so good that she had no need to return for additional treatment.

Mr Jack Halford

A hospital consultant had told Mr Halford that an operation might save his hearing, but, if unsuccessful, could result in complete deafness.

At his first healing treatment from Dr Chang, Jack Halford experienced the burning sensation inside his head which other patients have described. After one healing session his hearing was restored.

'When it was all finished, my hearing was perfect,' asserted Mr Halford. 'I could clearly hear whispering from some distance. It was incredible. Had I not experienced it myself I would not have believed it. You should have seen the face of the consultant at the Ear, Nose and Throat Hospital! He could not believe anything like this could happen. He said something about "an inexplicable miracle". He said there was no need for me to visit the hospital again as long as the "miracle cure" lasted.'

It has lasted. For the past seventeen years Jack Halford's hearing has been perfect.

Mark Hansford

At the age of twelve, Mark began to suffer chronic stomach pains. He was under constant medical care until 1968, when, at the age of fifteen, he applied to join the Royal Navy. He passed his tests and was accepted. Then he suffered a severe stomach upset. A barium meal showed he had a duodenal ulcer. Scars showed that he had suffered them previously. The Royal Navy withdrew acceptance of his services.

In June 1968, Mark suffered another severe attack of stomach pain. It was still his ambition to enlist in the Royal Navy and since the hospital medical methods had not given him relief from his complaint, he decided to try spiritual healing.

Dr Chang performed a spirit operation upon him but warned him that healing would not be instantaneous. It would take some time to be effective and there would be recurrences of his pain from time to time. But each time it would be less frequent and less painful.

'After we left you on Sunday,' Mrs Hansford wrote to Leah on 19th July 1968, 'Mark had pain; also on and off all day Monday. We were not perturbed because you had warned us to expect it. On Tuesday and Wednesday he had one slight twinge each day. Yesterday, he was free of pain. If I could only put into words all we feel. Apart from the ulcer clearing up, he is a much happier boy and is getting his old energy back. Coming to you has meant a great deal, as you see if his trouble had persisted it would have greatly hindered his future prospects.'

Recently, Mrs Hansford informed me: 'In all fairness I must say that it has been necessary for Mark to visit the doctor from time to time. But this discomfort has only lasted a few hours. And it has only showed itself at times of stress and worry. And even then it was short-lived.'

*   *   *

I had often wondered how Leah Doctors feels when she is being 'controlled' by Dr Chang and being kept busy healing. She answered my question in a quite matter-of-fact manner:

'When Dr Chang takes over I just relax. It's as though I step aside and forget myself. He uses my brain, but my larynx is still normal. I'm only in a *semi-trance,* but that's enough for Dr Chang's personality to come through. I cannot alter anything Dr Chang says through my voice. His spirit power is very strong indeed. I cannot resist in any way, not have I ever tried to, as this goes against my own nature. Dr Chang gives me confidence to heal with his spirit power. That is how I know I am only an instrument in his healing work. I do not know what Dr Chang is going to say next. It just comes out spontaneously. My own mind is quite blank when Dr Chang is speaking.'

ABSENT HEALING

All human beings are different. None can be expected to respond in *exactly* the same way to medical and spiritual healing. Doctors know well that patients with the same complaint, who are given exactly the same treatment, will not always improve in health at the same rate. Some patients get well quickly, others stubbornly resist all medicines and injections; their illness lingers on everlastingly.

Dr Chang experiences this same uneven response with his patients. Some he can heal at a single healing session. Others require long and regular treatment, sometimes lasting many months, and in some cases even years. When patients visit Dr Chang he makes it very clear that it is important to continue healing treatment until he can tell them there is no need for more healing sessions.

But when Dr Chang gives absent healing, he is not present to impress this necessity upon his patients. Although Leah Doctors and Dr Chang have brought about remarkable successes through absent healing, some of the healings could have been much more effective if the patients had continued with absent healing treatment. Far too often, Leah and Dr Chang told me, distant patients feel so improved in health after absent healing has been given for a certain period of time, that they decide they have been cured. 'They stop writing to report progress or setbacks to us, and break the vital link that enables us to heal them from a distance. Then, later, if they become ill again, and the same symptoms return, they conclude that our healing treatment has been ineffective.'

Leah Doctors insisted that it is essential in absent healing that 'some kind of vibration contact' exists between the medium and the patient. This can be established through a telephone call or through letters. 'It can also be strengthened by vibrations of thought waves,' Leah added. She, therefore, asks all absent healing patients to 'tune in' by thought with her and Dr Chang, every evening at 10 pm. With many minds united at an agreed time, a powerful 'thought vibration for the good' is built up.

If it is thought that spending a few moments thought-concentrating every evening, and writing letters regularly while receiving absent healing, is boring and useless, some of the following examples may make the reader pause and think again.

Mr Docherty

On 5th February 1962, hospital X-rays showed that Mr Docherty had a lump on the left lobe of his right lung. Lung cancer was diagnosed. Mr Docherty was admitted to hospital on 9th February. He was operated upon on 12th March and discharged from hospital on the 31st. He was told by the surgeon that the growth had *not* been malignant. On 2nd April, he suffered such bad bouts of coughing that he was re-admitted to hospital. In the summer of 1962, his surgeon stated he had *malignant* lung cancer.

Mrs Docherty wrote to Leah Doctors asking for absent healing for her husband. Healing began at the beginning of August 1962. A fortnight later, Mrs Docherty reported to Leah:

'I have a good report about my husband. Since last week he hasn't been given any more tablets. On Tuesday, he was weighed and had gained four pounds in two weeks. Thursday he had his check-up at the hospital. The doctor said there's a big improvement since his last X-ray. He has to report back in six months.'

During a year of absent healing, Mrs Docherty reported a gradual but steady improvement. At the end of the year, Mr Docherty's X-rays showed that he did not suffer from lung cancer. He was discharged from hospital.

Ten years later, in 1972, he was in good health. He has had no return of lung illness. Neither Mr Docherty, nor his wife, have ever had direct personal contact with Leah Doctors. The 'vital contact' has been maintained through regular letter-reports and 'thought waves'.

Mrs A Albright

Mrs Albright requested absent healing for her daughter. She was ill and also suffering from an arm injury. Absent healing began on 28th September 1963. Mrs Albright wrote on 5th October: 'My daughter is almost well, thanks to you and Dr Chang. God bless you both. I am going to ask Dr Chang's help for a few more nights.'

In her letter, dated 18th October, Mrs Albright reported: 'My daughter looks so very well, and her arm is so much better, thanks to you and Dr Chang. God bless you both. I am contacting him at ten o'clock every night.'

Absent healing continued for a few more weeks at the end of which time Mrs Albright's daughter was reported in full health again.

Mrs Violetta Smith

The doctors had stated that Mrs Smith's sister, Mrs Blake, was suffering from an incurable cancer of the bowels. They had done all that could be achieved with the aid of medical knowledge. She had only a few weeks to live. She was bedridden and it was impossible for her to visit Leah Doctors' healing sanctuary. Mrs Smith asked Leah to provide absent healing, which began on 11th August 1964.

'I went to Blackpool on Sunday and I had a lovely shock when I saw my sister, Mrs Blake,' Mrs Smith wrote to Leah a week later. 'She looks a different woman. She said she can hear the healers in her bedroom and she's so very grateful. When I wrote to you last week we thought she had only a week or two to live. Now she is talking about when she will be able to come out and see us again. Her mouth, that was all twisted to one side, is normal again, and the pain is less. She has a tube inside her but she hopes they can take it out soon. I would like to be present when her doctor sees her. I could tell him such a lot. Although he is kindness himself, he cannot do what spiritual healing can do. . . .'

Mrs Smith continued writing weekly, reporting improvement in her sister's condition. Her last letter conveys a report of Mrs Blake's doctor, who said she had been 'miraculously cured'.

Mrs Ann Jarvis

Mrs Jarvis asked for absent healing in August 1964. Her letter of 24th August 1964 is self-explicit:

'I feel such a lot better. Last Friday I got a walking-aid from the Red Cross. It's marvellous that I can use it. Just a few weeks ago I could hardly stand. Now I can walk through the bungalow. Yesterday, I sat in front of the dressing-table to do my hair. It's the first time I've done this in such a long time. Apart from when I first got up in the morning, or when I am cooking, I can spend most of the time out of my wheelchair. I still drag my legs. But several times I've been able to move my feet correctly.

'This morning, when my husband wanted to help me out of bed, I told him I would stay in bed a little longer, and assured him I would be all right. I not only got up out of bed without his help, but I also put on my dress, stockings and shoes. Up till now it's been all I could do to slip my feet into slippers. Dr Chang is helping me enormously. I would not have believed it possible if I hadn't experienced this myself. I am so grateful to him. Everyone remarks how well I look and I feel such a lot better myself now I can get up and out of my wheelchair. I don't know how to thank you.'

Mrs A Howell

Within a week of receiving absent healing for a painful knee-joint for which she had been prescribed pain-relieving tablets, Mrs Howell wrote to Leah Doctors on 19th November 1964: 'I must say that there has been a great improvement in my knee condition, for this I must thank you and your friend. Please continue with this work.'

Mrs Howell was eventually completely healed.

Mrs G Woodgate

Cancer of the throat. Recommended for surgery, Mrs Woodgate's sister-in-law asked Leah Doctors for absent healing, on 12th March 1962. It began immediately with Mrs Woodgate's knowledge. She meanwhile postponed her surgical operation. When she reported again at King's College Hospital, on 23rd March, she was told her operation was no longer necessary. All symptoms of cancer of the throat had disappeared.

Mrs Gladys Ainsworth

Poor vision, sinus trouble, and pain in the neck. Doctors prescribed pain-killing drugs for the back since therapy had not been successful. For her sinus trouble she received 'washing out' at regular intervals. The doctors at the Eye Hospital could not improve her eye condition.

Mrs Ainsworth asked for absent healing in the spring of 1964. On 26th June 1964, she reported:

'My sight is *much* clearer, and the spots and bubbles are becoming less in number. The Eye Hospital have now said I can have my reading-glasses changed, but, in future, I must also wear glasses outside, which I have not done before. I am without glasses altogether at the moment as I have left the readers to be changed. The hospital were quite surprised at the change in my eyes.

'I am so glad Dr Chang is treating my sinus, too. I am really quite terrified of having to have them washed out again. My neck and back of my head are still hot, but it is lovely to see so much clearer. I have to return to the Eye Hospital in a month's time.'

On 11th November 1964, Mrs Ainsworth reported: 'My back has now started to improve, so I can move about better. In other ways I am fine, for which I have to thank you.'

Mrs Lilian Davies

Suffering severe pains in chest and stomach. Requested absent healing in September 1968. On 7th October, she reported: 'My heart is full of gratitude for the measure of relief I have felt from the terrible pains I have had in my chest and stomach. . . . I still feel a little weak (because I have not been able to eat) but I am much *better* since Dr Chang has stopped the pains. . . .'

Mr Albert Wash

Cancer of the stomach. Under medical care. His wife asked for absent healing in April 1970. On 26th November 1970 she wrote: 'I made arrangements for my husband to see the specialist in his case, and when he saw Albert he was surprised how well he looked and passed comments on it. He has reduced the amount of one lot of tablets which is a good sign in itself. Albert certainly looks quite well, he is eating and sleeping well and talking about going back to work in the New Year. . . .'

Absent healing continued, and after seven months Mr Wash resumed work in the new year of 1971.

Mr Arthur Shead

Sinus trouble. Sore eyes. Constant nose drip. Did not respond to antibiotics. Requested absent healing in May 1972. On 11th June 1972 he wrote: 'I am glad to inform you that there has been a definite improvement in my sinus condition but it still troubles me in the early morning a little. I would also like absent healing for my nerves which seem to have been very tattered lately, and I become very ratty and sometimes depressed. . . .'

Absent healing continued, Mr Shead's health was restored, and he was able to resume work. Three years after receiving absent healing, he is completely free of ill-health and still working.

Mr K Richards

Mr Richards requested absent healing for his wife. His letter of June 1972, reported:

'My wife had an appointment with the hospital doctor yesterday. He was amazed that a lesion at the back of the eye had healed 'by itself', and said 'that has never happened to me before, and you couldn't have faked the symptoms.'

'As the specialist in charge of the case died whilst Vickie was convalescing from their painful tests, and they had not yet appointed a replacement, they seemed to be at a loss what to do. However, they took seven X-rays which turned out wrong, took seven more, and although they wanted Vickie for more tests, they agreed in the end to another appointment on 1st June. Vickie told them if they could get rid of the headaches, the buzzing in the left ear and the horrible tiredness she gets at the slightest exertion, she would be fine.

'They also said there was no longer any sign of a detached retina mentioned in her medical reports, which was something she was told last time [before absent healing commenced]. . . . She still does not know of your absent healing although I very nearly told her last night.'

Mrs Richards was given absent healing for a few more weeks until she got better. Her husband then stopped writing to Leah. He no longer required spiritual healing for his wife.

Mrs Elizabeth Francis, Denmark

Extreme exhaustion, loss of weight and energy. Unresponsive to medical treatment. Her mother-in-law requested absent healing in September 1972. On 14th October 1972, she reported:

'One month ago you very kindly put our daughter-in-law's name, Elizabeth Francis, on your healing list. My husband and I have linked in prayer and called on Dr Chang for healing for her at 10 pm each evening. Please may I ask you to continue absent healing.'

Absent healing continued and Mrs Francis got better. Her mother-in-law then stopped writing to Leah, thus terminating the healing.

Mrs Alice Smith

Mrs Smith had been in medical care for a very long time and had been told her condition was incurable. She applied for absent healing at the end of February 1965. Six weeks later she wrote the following letter, dated 6 April 1965:

'When I first asked you to help me I had been unable to go outside for many months. My breathing was so difficult I could only move about the room slowly; my legs and feet swelled up and I was very depressed after being told again by my doctor that I was incurable.

'Now the swelling has gone down, I find it easier to breathe, and the fear of choking to death is lifted. Yesterday, I was able to walk outside and plant some seeds in my garden. I sleep better at night and am no longer depressed. I have much to thank you for. You are proving how the healing power of God can be used to help those who are hopeless.'

* * *

While investigating Dr Chang's absent healing results, I was handed a mountain of letters written by grateful patients expressing thanks for healing. It is difficult to decide which ones to include in this book. I have eventually given preference to those which convey the human story of the patient's illness.

Mr John Black

The following letter to Leah Doctors was written by Mr Black on 14th May 1966 – six weeks after he had asked for absent healing for his wife:

'Many thanks indeed to you, and the great Dr Chang. My wife, bless her, is now a much different woman. Instead of behaving like a truly demented creature, dancing around like a raving lunatic, talking a diabolical dialect to who knows what, she is a much changed woman, and looks it. Yesterday, she stayed in bed all day. She ate a bowl of soup and bread and butter. The day before she was undoubtedly visited by Dr Chang. Whatever it was that was troubling her, has certainly met more than its match. I never saw or heard anything like this. I only wish I could have seeen it clairvoyantly.'

Mrs Black was eventually reported to be fully recovered from her illness.

Mrs E Brewer

Mrs Brewer's Letter, dated 28th August 1966, reads:

'I feel I must write and tell you that since I wrote and asked for your advice, wonderful things are happening. You said life would get better and it most certainly is. I feel constantly uplifted, and I know this help is coming from spirits. I am thirty-six but looked forty-five. Now my health is better than it has ever been. My life is changed. Now I am constantly thinking of health, happiness and vigour instead of the misery I have known. Life is opening up in new and wonderful ways. I find that I can help others too. I am lifting myself up from the lowest to the highest point, and life is becoming wonderful. Good health is now my cup of tea and I am putting on weight, exactly as I wanted. I am looking forward to going where I want to be, to making the happy changes I have been hoping to make for months. I know I can do it, and I can and I will! I want to thank you for your help because

I know you must have set things going to bring all this about. So, thank you, and God bless you.'

Miss Winifred Monteath, CMB, SCM

Miss Monteath wrote to Leah Doctors after benefiting from absent healing. She is an ex-nurse, and practised midwifery for twenty-eight years. Her following testimony she entitled:

A TRIBUTE TO HEALING.

'I wish to thank Leah Doctors for the benefit which I have received these past few weeks. All my life I have suffered from chronic and acute bronchitis. A recent spell lasted four months, with copious sputum. Dr Chang treated this a few times, telling me it had laid dormant for years. Then, whereas the sputum lessened very gradually over a week before the next attack, on this occasion it was copious one day; the next day gone completely. This is nearly three weeks ago and I am still clear and am aware of an improvement in breathing.

Miss B Rowland

For six months Miss Rowland suffered excruciating pain in her side and back. Although she availed herself of all medical assistance, her condition did not improve.

In March 1967, Miss Rowland applied to Leah for absent healing. On 2nd May 1967, she reported her pain had eased greatly, and on 10th June she stated she had been healed.

Mrs Martha Zabadal, Australia

Mrs Zabadal's little daughter was gravely ill. She wrote to Leah Doctors in October 1967, pleading for absent healing. On 14th November 1967, she reported: 'To let you know, my little daughter starts to show a little improvement. I can't express our thanks. Please continue to help her with spiritual healing. . . .'

Absent healing was continued and Mrs Zabadal wrote again on 26th January 1968: 'I let you know my little daughter starts to show big improvement. Perhaps in short time will be able to walk and talk and play. I know it won't be easy, but with your help I am sure it will be reached in time.'

Absent healing was continued and Mrs Zabadal's little daughter was completely healed.

Malcolm Bladon

Malcolm Bladon was under the care of a hospital specialist. He was suffering from tuberculosis of the lungs and chest. He had received continuous medical attention for five months but his condition was steadily deteriorating. His mother applied for absent healing in early December 1967. On 17th December that year she reported: 'After five months of living with it we can relax from some of our tension. The specialist said our Malcolm's condition is a miracle. He sees him again in February.'

On 7th January 1968, Mrs Bladon wrote: 'Our son Malcolm makes good progress. Really now – only us who know – one would never think anything had been wrong. Still, we must carry on with our efforts.'

On 28th January 1968, she wrote: 'He seems to be in good shape now, and no pain. He goes for a check-up in hospital in February. Thank you for what you have done.'

A letter dated 11th February 1968, stated: 'His hospital check-up last Tuesday was good. Beyond anything we could have expected eight months ago. We thank you for your part in this.'

Absent healing continued until Malcolm was healed.

Mr N Nethercott

Mr Nethercott had been ill and in pain for three years. Medical attention was unable to give him relief. His inability to work had plunged his family into dire economic straits. He asked for absent healing in April 1968. On 21st April, he reported:

'Thank you for your help. Here is my first report since I wrote to you for help. There has been a big improvement in my health. Although I now have very little pain, please continue with Absent Healing. I have had this illness for more than three years and I know it is a slow job to get rid of it. But I am very pleased at the results and once again I thank you very much for all you are doing. I feel sure I will soon be able to go back to work and give my wife and family a good home.'

Absent healing continued until the patient reported he was in good health again and back at work.

Mr J Stewart

Mr Stewart was dying of cancer. His daughter Ann asked for absent healing for him. Her letter, dated 7th January 1969, reported:

'I'm absolutely amazed at the difference in his condition. He was extremely ill and had given up all hope of recovering. He is now looking forward to returning to work. His outward body looks perfect. He still has the shaking of his body occasionally, but he is in perfect shape. He's stopped vomiting, etc. He has to go to hospital next Monday for blood tests and an examination. The blood test is to see if the red cells are still all right. I shall contact his family doctor to see what the local hospital report says about his X-rays. My father – with all his weight loss – now looks a very good colour, and is eating very well.

'I pray that your good work will continue, not only for my father, but for everyone who needs help. I'm sorry, but when I first wrote to you, I suppose having had no occasion to see any spiritual healing, I wondered if you could even ease his condition to allow him a little rest. I never dreamed the results could be so marvellous. You've no idea what it was like to know a dreadful secret – I couldn't tell my mother about it. So I'm even sleeping better myself, thanks to you. Needless to say, I will never forget your kindness. I only hope I can try to help other people by telling them about all this and making them believe.'

Mr Stewart was a patient who offered resistance to spiritual healing. Absent healing had to be persisted with for months. But eventually, he was completely healed.

Mrs J Malton

Mrs Malton's letter of 2nd November 1969, stated: 'Please continue healing for my bladder and internal condition. I am feeling stronger now and have more control than before the healing began. My stomach has less tension and is not so swollen and hard. I am feeling much happier and comforted by Dr Chang's nightly visits. Please say "thank you" to him. Will you please convey my sincere thanks to him.'

Mr J Finlayson

It is easy to forget that minor ailments can provoke a great deal of misery and suffering. A healthy man who has a raging tooth-ache probably suffers more agony than people who are seriously ill.

Mr Finlayson awoke each morning choking as the catarrh clotted in his throat. His tongue was so tender and inflamed that even eating was extremely painful. He'd endured this condition for five months when he made an appointment for spiritual healing. Leah couldn't see him at once but, at the beginning of October 1963, she wrote that she would give him absent healing until 26th October, when she would see him for direct contact healing.

On 8th October 1963, Mr Finlayson wrote to Leah: 'I am now feeling appreciably better, both physically and mentally; and am very grateful to your spirit physician Dr Chang for his administering to me the divine healing power. If you could convey to him my deep thanks I should be glad. Please accept my renewed thanks for your prompt help and kindness, for which I am indeed deeply grateful.'

Mr Finlayson wrote again on 15th October 1963: 'I am glad that this week I am able to report definite progress in regard to the morning clot of catarrh. It had choked me each morning when I got up and has persisted for at least five months. Four mornings ago it was as bad as it has ever been. But three mornings ago I awakened, and on arising was staggered to find no trace of what had become an abnormal normality. The same thing happened yesterday morning, and again today. It's as if a tap has been suddenly turned off. You can imagine how happy I have felt as a result of this transformation. My tongue also appears to be steadily improving; although progress here is slower, nevertheless it appears to be steady.'

On 22nd October 1963, Mr Finlayson wrote: 'I am now feeling very much better to what I was when I wrote to you. My tongue is very much improved and troubles me rarely. The catarrh clot in the mornings, although now has returned, it is much smaller, and only occurs irregularly. I am deeply grateful to Dr Chang and yourself for the valued help you have given me. I look forward to meeting you in person.'

Mr Finlayson made the journey from Scotland to London for his healing session. Subsequent to it he wrote to Leah: 'It is now a fortnight since I saw you in London, but I felt it would be better to allow a longer time than a week before writing to you. Now I can say thanks to the healing Dr Chang and yourself have given me. I feel appreciably better with regard to the three things for which you laid on hands, my tongue, the upper throat and catarrhal congestion, and the swelling on my knee. These three parts are considerably improved, especially my tongue which appears to be almost wholly better. For all your efforts on my behalf I do thank you most deeply.'

Absent healing treatment of Mr Finlayson continued until he was healed. Nine years later he did not report any recurrence of any of these illnesses.

Mrs Mary Turner, New Zealand.

Leah Doctors received a letter from Mr Turner asking for absent healing for his wife. She was gravely ill and her condition had not improved despite long medical attention. Two weeks after absent healing commenced, Mr Turner wrote: 'I wish to thank you for putting my wife on your absent healing list. I have much pleasure in saying she has derived much benefit, and the pain she had has lessened considerably.

Her stomach is much better and the pains in her back are not so severe. She is getting on well.'

Mrs Turner eventually terminated absent healing. She was cured.

Mrs R Stone

In January 1970, Mrs Stone requested absent healing to relieve her of stomach pains, palpitations of the heart, and breathlessness. Although she was receiving medical care, nothing alleviated her condition. She wrote to Leah Doctors again on 12th February 1970:

'I am glad to say my internal pains have been rarely felt since last writing to you. Also my palpitations and breathlessness are greatly improved. I am very grateful to you and your guide for helping me so much, and easing my worry about my health.'

In her letter dated 24th April 1970, Mrs Stone wrote:

'I have felt *much* better this last week or two. It is too good to be true. Please go on helping me to full recovery, and ask your guide to do so.'

Although there was a remarkable improvement in Mrs Stone's health and she was able to lead a painless and more or less normal life, Dr Chang was unable to cure her basic illness.

Mrs A Harding

On 2nd April 1970, Mrs Harding wrote to Leah Doctors: 'My husband reports his varicose veins are much better. The swelling has gone down and has not occurred again. He is also in less pain than previously.'

Absent healing was continued until Mr Harding was completely healed.

Mr W Wainwright

Mr Wainwright applied for absent healing in January 1970. He wrote a week after it commenced, on 26th January 1970, to Leah: 'I am pleased to tell you that I have not had any vascular spasms for the past four days. I still feel that the blood is not yet flowing freely to my brain, but I hope it will soon be cleared up. Thank you and Dr Chang for your efforts on my behalf. God bless you both.'

In his letter dated 13th February 1970, Mr Wainwright reported: 'I am pleased to say that I have had no vascular spasms for the past three weeks. I am returning to work next Monday.'

Mr S Wright

Mrs Wright requested absent healing for her husband in April 1970. Healing commenced, and Mrs Wright wrote the following letter on 18th April 1970:

'Thank you very much for all your help. My husband has improved tremendously in the last week. His headaches and leg aches have gone completely and his back is much better. He is extremely grateful. His doctor is amazed at his sudden recovery and has signed him off work for another fortnight, saying that only time now will make him better. Will you please continue helping? Please thank your Guide Dr Chang, and ask him if he will continue the healing as long as he thinks it is necessary.'

Mr Wright was soon restored to health.

Mrs Smith

Mrs Smith decided to seek spiritual healing for her husband when it was clear that he did not respond to medical treatment. She wrote to Leah in May 1970, requesting absent healing for Mr Smith, and a month later, on 9th June 1970, she was able to write the following:

'I feel I must write to you again to thank you as I do each night in prayer, both you and your Guide, Dr Chang. I thank you for the healing miracle, which has, and still is, taking place with my husband.

'It is wonderful, yet unbelievable, to see him as he tends to his greenhouse, and his plants, and attempts simple jobs which he thought he would never do again. He still has pins and needles in his right hand, but he is able to use the hand more and more as each prayer is answered. His right knee, and just above and below it, feel, as he says, *'as though fastened tightly with rubber bands',* and have no feeling. But he is now walking better, with very little trace of a limp.

'His whole personality is changing. He used to be hard and bitter; understandable after the hard knocks life has dealt him; but now a kindness and gentleness, even humility, is beginning to show itself. It is simply wonderful.'

Mr Smith was restored to almost normal health.

Mrs B Sellars

Mrs Sellars was a diabetic whose illness was kept in check by daily insulin intake. She wrote to Leah Doctors on 26th June 1970: 'I would like to thank you and your guide for the absent healing I am receiving for diabetes. I attended the hospital this week and they reduced the insulin by one half. I don't have to attend for another three months, which to me is marvellous. I do thank God and all helpers, including yourself.'

Mrs A Clarke

Mrs Clarke wrote to Leah from the Victoria Hospital in mid-June 1970, asking for absent healing. She wrote again on 23rd June 1970:

'Thank you and Dr Chang for the healing. When the doctor came round this morning he was a truly bewildered man, and naughty me was laughing to myself. He said to Sister: 'I cannot make it out. The state of those legs when she came in was that it would take at least eight weeks to get rid of the fluid. But there is no need now to have that right leg in bandages. Just massage it. If the left one gets on as well, she can get up at the end of the week to see what standing on them does.' So you can well guess how I appreciate your healing. And as soon as I can when I get home, I will be over to you for contact healing for where the root of the trouble is. Then maybe it will never start up again.'

After being discharged from hospital, Mrs Clarke received contact healing which cured the root cause of her illness.

Mrs M Boreham, South Africa

Mrs Boreham asked for absent healing for a variety of complaints in August 1970. She wrote to Leah again in September 1970:

'You will be pleased to hear of my good progress. (1) I am not able to say if the cataract in my eye has changed in any way but I can definitely say that my general eyesight is clearer and brighter. (2) I have had only one attack of night cramp when I had to get out of bed and walk around. But the attack was not one of the worst kind and it didn't last very long. (3) My slipped disc is quite a bit better and I feel I must add I generally feel much calmer, steadier and very hopeful. Needless to say I am very grateful to you and Dr Chang. I have felt twice that Dr Chang was near and helping me.'

Mrs Boreham wrote again – on 25th September 1970:

'You will be pleased to learn that I am progressing favourably. I only had one tiny cramp once, and my back is less painful, and my general eyesight is very good; as for my cataract, I don't know. The other thing is the haemorrhoids – "Percy the Pile" I call it. It has completely disappeared – unhonoured and unsung. I am surprised and delighted. Can I ask for spiritual healing for my husband who has very bad arthritis in his hands? I haven't told him anything about this question or about myself.'

On 17th October 1970, Mrs Boreham sent this report:

'Now for my last report. EYES: Very much better. I must explain that when I first had the cataract, my glasses were no good to me. The oculist was unable to give me anything more helpful. But now I am using my glasses and can read the newspaper. I thank God for Dr Chang's help and yours, dear Mrs Doctors. CRAMP: Also very much better. During this past week I have had no night cramp at all. BACK: Still improving. I must also tell you that with the disappearance of my piles, my inner works seem better. Please keep giving my husband spiritual healing for his arthritis. I have not told him anything and he has not mentioned improvement. But on the other hand – he hasn't said – as he sometimes does – *"my hands are so painful today"* so maybe that is the first healing step.'

On 3rd March 1971, Mrs Boreham wrote:

'I hardly ever get cramp these days and in consequence I have a restful sleep. My back is much better and the ankle ulcer is almost healed. Despite all this improvement in every way, I want to continue with your and Dr Chang's help – especially for my eyes.'

Mrs Boreham's final letter of 6th July 1971, stated: 'I am pleased to say that both my husband and myself are very satisfied with your healing.'

Mr C Burt

Mr Burt wrote on 13th March 1971, to Leah Doctors: 'I am pleased to report that my back has fully recovered, and I can now be taken off the absent healing list. I am indeed grateful for your kind and loving service, and for the healing administrations of Dr Chang from spirit.'

Mr L Cooray

On 15th January 1971, Mr Cooray wrote to Leah: 'I am grateful to you and Dr Chang for absent spiritual healing. The bronchial catarrh has disappeared; also my weakness has gone. Thank you.'

Mrs Estelle Carpenter, Ohio, USA

Mrs Carpenter wrote on 25th July 1971: 'The growth in my left eye is gradually disappearing and there is much less soreness. Thank Dr Chang again and again.'

Mrs Carpenter was eventually healed.

Mr A Richards

Mr Richards was suffering from an internal ulcer that was bleeding. He was scheduled to undergo a surgical operation when he wrote to Leah Doctors asking for absent healing. After healing began, he wrote on 24th August 1971: 'Re my ulcer trouble. I am pleased to say I am much better and the bleeding has stopped.'

Mr S Stone

This patient received absent healing at the request of his wife. He was elderly and his doctors did not believe he could recover from a cancerous growth. However, Mrs Stone wrote on 10th October 1971, to Leah: 'A good report regarding my husband. No headaches, no sickness and no exhaustion; only the tiredness that is normal for a man of his age. He looks much better, and for the last two days has looked even younger. I do hope we can keep this up.'

On 31st October 1971, Mrs Stone wrote the following: 'A lovely report this week. My husband has been extremely well all this week and eating well; the same food as I do. Which previously he couldn't. He says he feels younger, and we both thank Dr Chang and yourself.'

Unfortunately, Mrs Stone's hopes were dashed. Despite continued intense absent healing, her husband stopped benefiting from Dr Chang's ardent efforts. When it was evident that Mr Stone had ceased to respond to absent healing, his wife discontinued writing to Leah.

Mrs A Palfrey

Three weeks after asking for absent healing, Mrs Palfrey wrote to Leah – on 3rd March 1972: 'I would like you to know that my health continues to improve. There have been no palpitations for two weeks, the pain in my head has lessened, also the swelling of my stomach is going down.'

Mrs E Wardell

Mrs Wardell applied for absent healing at the age of fifty, in July 1972. She had been chronically ill and in the care of doctors since the age of three. In 1969, in addition to other complaints, she suffered a minor stroke which paralysed her face and shoulder. Mrs Wardell wanted to try absent healing but had no great hopes it would prove more successful than all the medical treatment she had received over the years.

Within a week of receiving absent healing she reported: 'I feel very, very much easier and my pain is completely gone.'

After four months of absent healing she wrote: 'It is really out of this world that in only four months Dr Chang and Leah Doctors succeeded in improving my condition, very, very drastically – something medical care could not bring about all my life.'

Mrs Wardell was confident her health would improve until she could lead an active and pain-free life. When I spoke with Dr Chang about Mrs Wardell's case, he said: 'Mrs Wardell is reacting to my healing rays treatment extremely well. But it will be a long time before I get her back to normal, or near-normal, health.'

From other records of Dr Chang's healings I know he does not make optimistic predictions unless he is confident he can keep his word.

Mr A Marshall

In August 1972, Mr Marshall asked for absent healing to save him from surgery to cure his piles. On 18th August 1972, he wrote: 'I am pleased to say there is a slow, steady improvement in my general condition, and in the piles.'

But Mr Marshall's optimism was unjustified. Spiritual absent healing could not do what a surgeon's skill could. As he did not achieve anything by writing these letters to Leah Doctors, he discontinued absent healing.

Mr D Sandham

Mr Sandham suffered from piles and had severe diarrhoea. He had been under the doctor for some time, using ointments and taking medicines. His condition didn't improve. His piles were bleeding and extremely painful. Diarrhoea made him weak. His shop was his livelihood and like many small businessmen he could not afford to take time off to undergo a surgical operation. His wife wrote to Leah Doctors asking for absent healing. After this commenced, she wrote, on 6th September 1972, the following letter:

'I am really pleased, to tell you that in his own words there has been a *"noticeable improvement"* in my husband's condition. He noticed this improvement last Thursday – the day you wrote to us – and it has continued since. The piles that had bled had ceased to bleed at all, although he is still aware of them. But yesterday, he said, he did not bleed again. This compared with previously is an improvement in itself. The diarrhoea has toned down quite considerably – he still has some trouble with this, but it does seem to be responding, at least I think so. All in all, though not exactly cured yet, he does seem to be on the way to being cured and I am truly thankful.'

Absent healing continued until Mrs Sandham stopped writing, obviously believing a cure had been affected.

Mr D Martin

Mr Martin could not walk properly because of a diseased right foot and left knee. The doctors were also amputating his right forearm. His left arm was amputated in 1970. He wrote to Leah Doctors in June 1972, asked for absent healing and described his condition. His right hand and forearm were covered with blotchy skin growths that the doctors diagnosed as cancer. Mr Martin wrote again on 23rd September 1972:

'You will be happy to know that my right hand is really progressing, and is at last so much better. That what was thought to be the cancer area and is now almost healed and there is no longer any purple flesh. The skin is growing normally, thank God.

'Last Monday I saw a lady specialist whom I had not seen since June and she was amazed. She confessed that by now she thought I would have lost my forearm. I see my own specialist again on Monday. The last time I saw him, he was very pleased.

'In myself I feel quite well and have more energy than was the case. I am still not able to walk well and the right foot and the left knee are the troublemakers. But I know you will please remember these as well as all my blood, skin and right hand, please. It is difficult to thank you and the guide for all you have done. In June and July there was no hope of saving the hand as far as the doctors were concerned. But now, all being well, there is no question of an operation. And for this, we sincerely thank you and your helpers.'

On 11th October 1972, Mr Martin wrote:

'I am very pleased to say that in myself I am much better, and have more energy, the walking is a little better, and there is less pain in the right foot, and the left knee is a great deal better, and for this I do thank you sincerely; my general skin is fairly well at the present time.

'As to my right hand, I think we can say the miracle continues; there is clearly an improvement, and the raw area is less, and around looks more healthy; the specialist is very happy over it. It is less sore, but still hurts at times, but nothing as it did .... During the past three months the hand has healed wonderfully, and certainly should not have done.

'I wonder, please, if you and your guides will please take my mother on as a patient, as she certainly needs help.

'About four years ago, she started with what is called mid-ears disease; this is a condition of the inner ear, and causes a person to be violently dizzy, and sick, vomiting very often, rather like sea-sickness; it is caused by the nerves. It was the left ear that was infected, as mother went deaf in the left ear, and has for the past four years had a loud hissing noise in the left ear, all the time.

'The dizziness and vomiting stopped after a few months but the deafness and hissing remained, but if her nerves are upset then she starts to be ill again, and I think that the worry all this Summer over my hand has caused her to be ill again. (She started to be ill in the first place a few weeks after I lost my left arm through the cancer there.)

'She has been unwell for the past fortnight or so and her nerves have been very bad indeed, and yesterday she had to spend the day in bed, this morning when getting up for breakfast she fainted over breakfast and was very ill for a time, and then vomited. She is a little better now but of course in bed.

'I am sorry to have written such a long letter, but I thought it best to explain in detail to help you and your Healing Guide. I do hope that you will be able to help her, please, and to help this nerve condition. She has had such a dreadful life in many ways, it seems a shame to have this now.'

Absent healing for Mr Martin and his mother continued with determined intensity. It was thus a shock to Mr Martin to learn that the seeming healing of the skin cancer on his hand and forearm did not endure. Throughout the period absent healing was given the patient co-operated with the spirit doctor and his medium. But his condition steadily deteriorated until his medical consultants decided upon surgery. Mr Martin's hand and arm were amputated! So Mr Martin and his mother regarded absent healing to be useless and have stopped writing to Leah Doctors.

MEDICAL GLOSSARY

Compiled by Dr Michael F Kirkman

ACUPUNCTURE – historical method of treatment of diseases using scientific puncture of parts of the body by thin steel needles of variable diameter and length or by electrical means. The place of puncture is determined by experience and study of the parts concerned, which are not necessarily the location of evidence of the disease.

AMNESIA – loss of memory often following severe shock, head injury, or emotional disturbance.

ANAEMIA – defect of the red blood cells from various causes of which iron deficiency, defective blood formation, other nutritional defects, and excessive destruction or defects of bone marrow formation of the red cells are the most important.

ANTIBIOTICS – anti-bacterial agent made from natural micro-organisms or by biochemical laboratory synthesis.

APPENDIX – a small blind-ended sac situated at lower end of large intestine; appendicitis – inflammation of same. This inflammation can be sudden, ie, acute, or 'grumbling'; or relapsing, ie, chronic. The causation is not specifically universal but is probably due to infection superimposed on an obstruction of the vestigial sac.

ARTHRITIS – inflammation of a joint or joints leading to swelling, pain, and ultimately stiffness, resulting from injury, rheumatism, gout, or gonorrheal or tuberculous process. When chronic, with deformity and inability to move, it is known as osteo-arthritis.

ASTHMA – recurrent intermittent disorder consisting of incapacitating paroxysms of difficult breathing due to narrowing of breathing tubes; caused by allergic, infective, psychological factors.

BARIUM ENEMA and MEAL – a heavy white barium sulphate substance which is opaque to X-rays and taken by mouth (meal) or by instilling via anus (enema). The result is the showing of outlines of stomach or intestinal profiles and cavities and used in diagnosis of disease of these parts.

BENIGN – see cancer.

BLOOD–COUNT – the determination of the number and kind of red and white blood cells in a given volume of blood in relation to the normal average values.

BRONCHITIS – inflammation of virus and bacterial origin of breathing tubes or of heart origin leading to cough and debility.

CANCER/TUMOUR – aberrant unnatural growth of body tissue of any kind, often of unknown origin and causation, but with familial, age determinant and external physical and chemical contributory factors. Typed as:

(a) BENIGN – a cancer growing in one location and producing pressure and other local effects but not invading neighbouring parts. Usually does not recur after total removal surgically; but may develop into malignant tumour later in life or if irritated. May sometimes be indistinguishable from malignant.

(b) MALIGNANT – tissue growth which invades and destroys surrounding parts and spreads to other disassociated parts of the body and grows there. Usually recurs after removal at original site or elsewhere.

CATARACT – opacity, following gradual senile degeneration of crystalline lens of eye and leading to loss of vision.

COLITIS – inflammation of part of large intestine characterised by multiple daily motions of fluid stools resulting in emaciation, weakness, and anaemia.

CORNEA – clear membrane in front of eye lens.

CRAMP – painful spasm of muscles and internal organs, usually of nerve-centre origin or external physical conditions, often at night.

CYST – hollow, encapsulated sacs of fluid or tissue material not malignant.

DIABETES – constitutional disorder due to lack of secretion of pancreatic insulin hormone which results in the accumulation of sugar in blood and urine above normal and so affects body functioning; diabetic – sufferer from diabetes, who is receiving supplementary insulin by daily injection.

DIAGNOSIS – medical and scientific terminological definition of patient's condition of disease which determines the course and extent of rational medical and surgical or psychiatric treatment.

DIOPTER – describes scientifically the focusing power of the lens required to correct vision in spectacles.

DISC – vague term describing a condition of spaces between the vertebrae of spine indicating causation of pressure on nerves emanating from spine which results in pain. This pain is local and also radiates down legs especially on movement. Condition known as sciatica or slipped disc.

DISSEMINATED SCLEROSIS – disease of brain and spinal cord which is slowly progressive, resulting in increasing state of limb tremors and paralysis. Unknown specific causation and unsatisfactory in treatment.

DIVERTICULITIS – inflammation of numerous extra pockets attached to intestines, often of hereditary nature and affecting body by absorption of poisonous inflammatory products.

DUODENAL ULCER – localised sloughing of part of intestinal wall just beyond the stomach resulting in pain, internal bleeding and failing health. May have stress origin and may perforate or become cancerous.

DYSPEPSIA – stomach pain and discomfort following eating. Common in nervous individuals and accompanied by regurgitation of sour acid material and chest pain (heartburn) and often a sign of stomach ulcer.

EPILEPSY – condition of intermittent sudden convulsions and/or loss of consciousness which results from disordered brain function.

FIBROIDS – tumour of the womb, consisting of masses of muscle fibres leading to menstrual irregularity and excessive loss of blood during extended periods.

GALL BLADDER – a sac adjacent to the liver which collects liver products, concentrates them, and secretes them into the intestine as bile.

GAMMA-RAYS – electromagnetic waves generated and used in the destruction of cancerous tissue.

GLANDS – organs of body which secrete essential substances.

GLAUCOMA – disease of the eye, resulting from increased pressure in the eyeball which destroys visual nerves and vision.

HAEMORRHAGE – external or internal bleeding.

HAEMORRHOIDS (piles) – varicose veins around the lower end of bowels, causing pain, discomfort, and bleeding.

HERNIA – protrusion of bowel through abdominal wall, usually in groin region.

HIATUS HERNIA – stomach protrusion through diaphragm into chest cavity.

HYPNOSIS – temporary induced condition of mind leading to enhanced and often permanent suggestibility.

HYSTERIA – overaction of body nervous and emotional states due to genuine or self-induced crises.

INFANTILE PARALYSIS (Poliomyelitis) – virus infection affecting nerves of brain and spinal cord.

INFECTION – invasion of body tissues by disease producing bacteria, viruses and fungi – usually transmittable to others.

INFLUENZA – virus infection producing 'cold-like' symptoms.

INSULIN – pancreatic gland secretion which controls body sugar and energy levels. Absence or reduction leads to diabetes. Can now be synthesised and injected.

KYPHOSIS – abnormal curvature of spine.

LABYRINTH – part of internal ear, concerned with hearing and controlling body balance and orientation.

LEUKAEMIA – cancer of white blood cells, acute or chronic, of unknown specific cause and usually fatal.

MACULA – point of internal eyeball.

MALIGNANT – see cancer.

MEMBRANE – thin cellular tissue bounding organs.

MÉNIÈRES DISEASE – ear disease characterised by sudden giddiness, headache, deafness, and ringing in the ears – due to labyrinth failure.

MIGRAINE – condition of recurrent intense headaches.

MYOPIA – short sight due to wrong focus of eye lens.

OSTEO – ARTHRITIS – see arthritis.

PANCREAS GLAND – abdominal gland secreting insulin.

PAROTID GLAND – salivary gland in cheek in front of ear – seat of mumps infection.

PERITONEUM – membrane lining abdominal cavity.

PHLEGM – infected sputum from lungs.

PILES – see haemorrhoids.

PHLEBITIS – painful inflammation of veins – usually leg veins.

POLIOMYELITIS – see infantile paralysis.

PROLAPSE – protrusion of bowel or womb displaced towards exterior.

PSYCHOLOGY – study of mind and its functioning in relation to hereditory and environmental factors.

PSYCHOSOMATIC – disease condition of body related to mental or emotional states affected by environmental factors.

RADIUM TREATMENT – treatment by electromagnetic rays.

RETINA – light sensitive part of eye.

RHEUMATISM – old term describing painful joints and muscles.

SCLEROSIS – thickening, hardening, leading to loss of function of tissues.

SINUSES – air-containing cavities around and communicating with nasal system and often inflamed and painful.

STOMACH and STOMACH ULCER – see duodenum and dyspepsia.

STROKE – bleeding due to ruptured blood vessel, into brain tissue areas which results in body paralysis especially in limbs and face.

THROMBOSIS – clotting of blood within the blood vessels.

TINNITUS – ear noises heard without external noise causation.

TUBERCULOSIS – infection of lungs, bones, joints and other organs with tubercle bacilli.

TUMOUR – see cancer.

ULCER – defect in surface of skin or internal organ.

ULTRA-VIOLET RAYS – electromagnetic waves of sun or artificially created by lamps and leading to increasing pigmentation of skin and burning.

UTERUS – womb.

VARICOSE VEINS – abnormally dilated, elongated, and tortuous alterations of veins of lower leg and anal region (piles).

VERTEBRA – one of the bones of the spine.

VERTIGO – subjective feeling of rotation, unsteadiness, or haziness of vision accompanied with anxiety state.

WART – small tumour – benign perhaps – of various origin on skin or mucuous membrane surfaces.

X-RAYS – photosensitive rays showing internal organs of body as photographic negatives when passed through body. Used in diagnosis and treatment.

INDEX